INQUIRY-BASED COACHING:

The Power of Zerospace

Dr. Pedro Cortina & Tania Fierro, MA

INQUOS Publications
Vancouver, Canada

Copyright © 2022
by Dr. Pedro Cortina & Tania Fierro, MA

All rights reserved. No part of this publication may be reproduced, distributed, or transmitted in any form or by any means, or stored in a database or retrieval system without the prior written permission of the authors.

INQUOS Publications
Vancouver, B.C
www.inquos.com

ISBN 9798372121768

Important Notice to Reader

All content and practices in this book are presented as an invitation into the exploration of our internal world for the purposes of self-discovery, personal inquiry, and ultimately inner freedom.

If readers choose to engage with the content and practices presented in this book, they do so under their own responsibility. The content and practices in this book are not intended for providing advice, diagnosis, prescription, treatment, or cure for any condition, nor do they address any specific situation.

Naturally, individuals remain wholly responsible for their own understanding, experience, and actions. Appropriately qualified, licensed, or professional support should be sought to address particular needs.

Inquiry-Based Coaching

*For all who seek
boundless inner
freedom*

INQUIRY-BASED COACHING:

The Power of Zerospace

Index

Origins 11
Introduction 15

I The Spirit of Inquiry 19
1: The Four Aspects of the Spirit of Inquiry 21
2: Foundations of the Practice 25

II Zerospace 27
1: What is Zerospace? 29
2: What Gets in the Way of Zerospace? 33
3: The Puppeteer Elephant in The Room 39
4: Innocence 45
5: IBC: Dissolving the Algorithm 47
6: Is Your Zero, Their Zero, My Zero? 53
7: Zero is Zero is Zero 55
8: Responsibility and Zerospace 59

III Inquiry-Based Coaching 65
1: Ease of Transformation 67
2: Finding Clarity for Yourself 71
3: The Power of Open-Ended Questions 75
4: Identifying the Issue 79
5: The IBC Questions 85
6: Getting to Zerospace with IBC 91
7: Answering the IBC Questions 95
8: IBC and Parts 113
9: IBC and The Spiral 117

10: How do You Know When You're in Zero? 119
11: I Will Never Get to Zero 121
12: Depth, Honesty, and Consistency 125
13: Zero-Expansion 129
14: Living from Zero 133

IV Practicing IBC 135
Eight Examples from 10 to Zero 137
1: I Need Something from the Outside 139
2: I Need to Know Where He Is 155
3: My Partner 165
4: I Lost Myself 177
5: He Never Cared About Me 189
6: I Feel Like a Nervous Little Girl 209
7: I Want to Stop Overthinking Things 227
8: I Can't Breathe at Night 239

Testimonials 255

Organizational Results 263

Innerland Institute 265

About the Authors 269

Origins

This book was born from decades of profound and sincere exploration into the nature of both human condition and human potential. Tania and I have been sharing interests and passions since we met when we were in high school back in Mexico City in the late 1980's. As young people, we seemed to be the ones not simply interested in the surface of things but often the ones asking the 'unaskable' and exploring the unanswerable (or so people said). We were the ones trying to live the deeper experiences of life and the ones willing to make the adventurous inner journeys.

Adolescence came and went and, as we were growing out of it, our paths became even more strongly united, leading us to a clear and honest commitment to do everything possible to solve life's paradox, to solve the mystery of suffering, of inner alienation, and of existential longing.

In university we decided to dive deep into the mysteries and complexities of several Western and Eastern philosophies and their practice. After some time, we moved to Canada in the early 2000's to pursue a different life, engage in graduate education, and set up an institute with the aim of supporting people in their adventure towards inner alignment and understanding. We did this always with the aim of finding and *applying* what was as relevant and empirically transformative as possible.

As part of this process, we founded the Innerland Institute in 2003 and began offering individuals and groups several tools to address what was getting in the way of their passion, purpose, and inner alignment. For almost 20 years, we built a very successful practice offering one-on-one facilitation and coaching, as well as group immersions, retreats and workshops throughout North America and Europe. We also started expanding our offering at Innerland to serve businesses and organizations. We further developed the Inquiry-Based Coaching (IBC) model, which we were able to further adapt, test, apply and measure with extraordinary results.

Currently, at the Innerland Institute we offer IBC Certification programs for coaches and therapists as well as leadership development programs for organizations. We also offer short introduction courses as well long-term immersion programs for the general public including life-changing retreats in incredible locations. Finally, we also offer our two-year Innerland Institute Coaching certification program.

Inquiry-Based Coaching™ (IBC™) is a form of guided or self-driven internal exploration in which we:
1) Identify what is internally impeding our most extraordinary experience of life.
2) Explore how we *innocently* (yes, innocently) validate and justify the perceptional obstacles that sustain our limiting experience of life.
3) Explore the impact that this validation and justification has in our experience of life.

4) Deeply realize how this validation and justification of the obstacles drives us to miss extraordinary opportunities and resources that are practically and consistently available to us behind or beyond our limiting perception, and
5) Fully experience our life without unnecessary perceived limitations, dissolving those hard-to-crack patterns entirely as we embark on clear and sustained transformative action. This boundless space of inner freedom, clear action, accomplished potential and wholly aligned existence is what we call **Zerospace**.

In this book, we will invite you to join us in this adventure that has taken several decades and countless hours of profound exploration and commitment to actualize in a way where we can now share with the world. We deeply appreciate your interest in IBC and on your own profound and sustained personal transformation.

 In this book, we will explore in detail not only the IBC method but the result of its sustained practice: a space of inner alignment, clarity, understanding, connection, openness, joy, and compassion that as mentioned before we call **Zerospace**.

Valle de Bravo, Mexico
January 1, 2023

For a more detailed description of our professional background, a sample of testimonials and applied results in corporate environments, or more information about the programs we offer in IBC, please see the last chapter of this book, or visit innerland.com

Introduction

~

If there were a simple everyday practice that could radically transform your experience of life into an open, clear, connected, expansive, active and driven adventure (yet naturally compassionate and intrinsically loving), would you want to learn more about it?

~

> "If you look at **zero** you see nothing, but look through it, and you will see the world."
>
> Robert Kaplan

Zerospace *is a resulting inner experience of deep transformation and inner self-realization that is gained through a method we call* **Inquiry-Based Coaching (IBC)**.

In Zerospace, we live life as
a powerful experience of
compassion, understanding,
self-alignment, clarity, action,
joy, fulfilment, and love.

IBC is a set of 16 open-ended questions designed to transform our perception of life radically and persistently to transmute what is getting in the way of the most wholesome and joyful expression of ourselves.

In **part I** of this book, we will talk about the mindset that is needed to start our IBC exploration, we call it the five aspects of the Spirit of Inquiry

In **part II** we will focus and explore Zerospace in detail: What is it? What gets in the way of Zerospace? How do we sustain it? And more.

In **part III** of this book, we will explore the IBC method in detail as a methodology designed specifically to access Zerospace. What are the 16 questions? What is each question asking? How to answer each of them? And more.

In **part IV** of this book, we will explore the *practice* of IBC and how we conduct it. We will also share several transcripts of real IBC facilitations with eight different practitioners that ended up fully accessing Zerospace. In these transcripts, you will notice how practitioners address some of the most difficult and painful experiences in their lives and then transform these into their unique expression of clarity, understanding, compassion, love, and joy.

This book is a deeply honest and genuine attempt to deliver a simple, fully functional model of self-transformation in a truly grounded, practical, and wholly applicable way. May all who seek boundless inner freedom find the joy of Zerospace!

I

The Spirit of Inquiry

~

*To be curious is to be open, to be willing
to stretch the boundaries of our mind
and heart, to know that we have worlds
upon worlds to discover in
the book of Self.*

~

1

The Four Aspects of the Spirit of Inquiry

A mind that inquires is an open mind. A mind that seeks to manifest and embody understanding, compassion, clarity, insight, joy, connection, and fulfillment is an open mind. An open mind is something we cultivate with self-compassion and persistence.

To support an open and inquiring mind, we should cultivate the following:

1. A openness to be wrong about our worldview, our view of others and our view of self.

Please take a moment to explore genuinely how it would possibly benefit you to be willing to be mistaken about your own worldview? Especially about those repetitive painful patterns that you are tired of? Consider how this approach could allow you to become open and willing to see those reactive and hardwired internal mental/emotional algorithms that tend to hide well in plain sight.

Invite yourself to also explore what specific assumptions about the world, self or others you are willing to open about or be mistaken about. Why would you be willing? Because you might now have sufficient evidence that holding on to them hurts more than it serves, and that this holding does not really work for moving forward in life. Take a moment and experience the openness that comes from being willing to be wrong. Breathe, become still and notice.

2. A willingness to be genuinely curious.

Genuine curiosity becomes a true form of internal medicine to support the IBC process. To be willing to be mistaken naturally invites genuine curiosity, which implies moving into a space where we see what parts of us we do not really know and feel the desire to get to know. It is a space where the less we assume we know, the better.

As you practice IBC, we invite you to consider what aspect of the issue you are exploring, you are willing to be genuinely curious about. Take a moment to become aware of this. How does genuine curiosity feel in your body? Breathe, become still and notice.

3. A willingness to be genuinely vulnerable.

We hear this word a lot, but what does it really mean? It means to be willing to be fully honest with yourself and others about what is genuinely showing up for you, and to do so even if being fully honest with yourself produces anxiety or some other form of emotional discomfort. Being able to fully hold and receive the experience of what is truly alive in the moment, while also allowing in full understanding for any discomfort in your body to exist, is a true example of vulnerability.

Vulnerability is not about forcing yourself into feeling something artificial, or worse, presenting yourself as an overly sensitive person to fit a particular expectation of vulnerability. True vulnerability means becoming friends with the tenderness of what it is like to be in a space of not knowing, or not assuming, while holding everything that comes up from that in a space of self-compassion and acceptance.

What does it feel like to be vulnerable about a particular issue you are exploring? What emotions arise when you do so? Can you be patient, open and fully available with yourself? Invite yourself to become good at feeling, feeling it all, the ugly, the hard, the uncomfortable, instead of only looking to feel good while pushing or numbing your inner world in all kinds of ways (overworking, drinking, eating, the internet, social media, etc.).

4. A willingness to take responsibility for your assumptions.

Growth does not occur naturally in our comfort zones. Growth requires perspective, movement, stretching, testing, and knowing how to find your edge or becoming "edgy". In other words, growth requires exploring what is uncomfortable and then having a willingness to take responsibility for it.

We genuinely invite you to notice what this discomfort is trying to teach you and to take responsibility for it. What is it saying beyond your innocent reactivity and fear? Can you listen without pushing it away or into a corner? Can you give it the time, the space, and the understanding it needs? Can you stop the habit of resisting and invite allowing instead?

As we move forward, we invite you to cultivate these **four aspects of an open mind.**

2
Foundations of the Practice

From our experience, *there are three foundations that sustain deep and powerful transformation.*

1) The Goal – There needs to be a clear definition of the goal. In our case the goal is ***to recognize, relax into, and live from Zerospace***. Throughout the book, we will give extensive accounts of this goal through different perspectives. We will discuss what Zerospace is and what it is not; we will discuss how to access, sustain, and expand it, how to know when you are there and what to look for in terms of obstacles to access it. *Zerospace is the goal, and the goal is Zerospace.*

2) The Method – In the same way that there is a very clear definition of the goal, we also need a very clear definition of the practice. In this case, ***the practice is IBC***. Throughout the book we will explore how to practice IBC and how to identify a particular issue to bring to IBC. We will also discuss all the IBC questions and how (or from where) to answer them. We have also explored the five aspects of the inquiring mind that serve as prerequisites to be able to practice successfully.

3) The Community – *The third foundation of the practice is the community.* Through community, we recognize everyone that has an active interest in transforming their lives through the consistent practice of IBC. We have developed countless models of participating or being a part of the IBC practicing community. We will be happy to share more details about how we practice as a community and how we sustain the practice of others.

II

Zerospace

~

What would happen if most of what you negatively assume about self, other, and the world could be consciously resolved, so you find yourself free to live in a compassionate, non-judgmental, open, curious, clear, active, joyful and loving way?

~

1
What is Zerospace?

Zerospace is a personal experience of full alignment, wholeness, joy, peace, clarity, spontaneity and freedom that is accessible to everyone who is open to it.

In Zerospace, our actions are naturally clear, sustained, aligned, and accompanied by a profound sense of understanding of ourselves, others, and the world around us.

In Zerospace, we take responsibility of our lives by successfully seeing and transcending the repetitive and painful patterns, constraints, projections, anticipation, apprehensions, fears, assumptions, and doubts that are generally part of the natural human condition and therefore accompany us throughout our lives.

In Zerospace we fully align to an experience of life that is wholly supported and genuinely complete every moment of every day.

Many historical traditions have referred to this direct experience of existence, and in many cases this experience has been the origin or cornerstone of extraordinary philosophical and transformational movements around the world.

We have countless references to this experience in countless IBC practitioners around the world. In truth, when Zerospace becomes accessible by some form of a new approach, reframing or breakthrough methodology, it often becomes of extraordinary benefit and support for the people who practice it. It becomes a form of coming home, a remembering of our original alignment to the source of who we are.

Throughout history, accessing this space has often been experienced as a formidable feat, and we have no doubt that this has been the case, indeed. It was true for us throughout our first 20 years of searching for it without being able to access it as we do now.

The greatest feat though is not only to *access* but also to *stabilize* the direct experience of Zerospace. Stabilization of Zerospace is achievable with consistent practice, support, and perseverance. Finding Zerospace is half the journey; the other half is living from that space every day.

Again, Zerospace is an embodied experience of being where we are fully aligned, whole, and available. An experience of being where anxiety and fear are replaced with deep self-knowing and trust. An experience of being where clear action arises naturally and spontaneously. An experience of being where there is an inherent trust in the flow of things, where uncertainty becomes a place for possibilities and wonder instead of dread and anxiety.

2

What Gets in the Way of Zerospace?

This is a very important question. What is hiding the Zerospace experience from us, or limiting it for us? Well, in short, what hides Zerospace from us is *the mental projections and preconceptions that reactively inform our way of being in the world.* These preconceptions create narrow assumptions and experiences of ourselves, others, and the world.

These preconceptions are so numerous, efficient, reliable, and consistent that we end up creating internal alternative realities based on them and then begin innocently unknowingly living our lives from these alternative realities, inadvertently generating a great amount of suffering for ourselves and others.

We say *inadvertently* because almost everybody around us is unaware of this condition. It is so pervasive and common, so inherently ubiquitous that we just assume it to be the human condition. We grow up and learn about life and how to live it in an environment where this misalignment is considered a given, the norm or even the common expression of life.

This illusory alternative reality that we create *does* allow us to function and interact to sustain life somewhat efficiently. Even though we are surviving and figuring things out the best way we can as a species, we do so in a way that we are constantly experiencing confusion, misalignment and existential pain fueling conflicts and misunderstanding, as well as generating considerable anxiety, dread, and disappointment in ourselves and others.

As a species, from an evolutionary perspective, we have done a great job surviving and thriving. It is clear now that in addition to surviving and thriving, most of us also have the expectation of doing it in a **happy and fulfilling way**, yet we are finding this incredibly difficult to achieve. Being interested in and longing for happiness is great; nevertheless, our tight mental structures are focused mainly on the 'survival' part of the equation and not on the 'fulfilled, free and happy' part.

This problem simply means that from a very early age and probably all the way up to this moment in our lives, we have been running, nurturing, and internally solidifying an endless number of unconscious perceptional assumptions in the form of **untested internal algorithms** that support the 'survive and thrive' side of the equation only. These internal algorithmic models heavily influence and sometimes even fully run our lives.

INTERNAL ALGORITHMS

So, what is an ***algorithm***? We may have heard this term in the areas of mathematics, technology, coding, software development, etc. In the most basic of terms, an algorithm is *a simple rule* that is stated in this very clear format: "IF X, THEN Y". It is important to note that both X and Y need to be given a specific ulterior objective, goal, or agenda for the algorithm to work.

For example, when it comes to the goal of *safety*, IF "I see a red light" THEN "I stop". When it comes to the goal of *having good relationships*, IF "I see her/him upset" THEN "I listen to him/her". When it comes to the goal of *success*, IF "I work hard" THEN "I will make it".

So if the agenda behind our biological wiring is to survive as a species, then algorithms will look and sound something like this: IF "she/he raises their voice" THEN "I have to defend myself"; IF "he/she is kind and loving towards me" THEN "I feel protected and cared for"; IF "I feel afraid" THEN "I will freeze or not make a decision until I'm out of danger", etc. Algorithms assume a specific prior condition to determine, project, or foresee a future one tied to a particular agenda (in this case to survive, evolve, or create safety).

In the case of our internal experience, the assumption part of the equation happens almost instantly, and in many cases the reactive part of the equation immediately follows without any form of verification or even awareness. ***This instantaneous, un-verified, and un-tested assumption-to-reaction approach is the source of most of our interpersonal problems as well as our own experience of stress, anxiety and existential discontent.***

Our suggestion here though is not to entirely disqualify or pick a fight with the algorithm. This would only complicate things more and make the algorithms stronger and more reactive (see Curflexion: The Two for One Paradox*).* ***It is very important to understand that projective and protective algorithms are there for a reason***. They are a very efficient way for nature to champion its main goal: survive, evolve, and stay safe.

The downside of this survivalist approach is that projective algorithms (as efficient as they may be) are also the source of assumptions, imagined expectations, and outcomes that as we have said before *literally* create a form of abstract, un-tested, unvalidated, and unsubstantiated *alternative reality* that is not only consistently confusing but also demanding of our energy and attention for it to be able to sustain itself.

This demand for energy and attention takes away energy from deeper areas of our human potential such as self-awareness, openness, curiosity, understanding, clear action, drive, alignment, and a wholesome absence of fear. To show you the effects of this condition, we can do a simple ten-minute exercise:

THE ALGORITHM EXERCISE

On a piece of paper write the following statement:
"I am often concerned about/afraid of…"
Then let your mind add as many real examples as it can find. Write down everything you are often concerned about/afraid of that pops into your mind following that prompt for about 2 minutes.

After writing down as many issues as you can in 2 minutes, write down a new prompt that reads:
"I often really want…"
Then again, let your mind wonder and write down every want that comes up for just 2 minutes.

Finally, write down a third prompt:
I am often paralyzed/don't know what to do about…"
and again write what shows up for that prompt for 2 minutes.

After you finish the 6 minutes, take a breath, and read all the answers to your prompts. After reading all of them, close your eyes and ask yourself:

What percentage of your daily energy is invested in the anticipation, projection, or management of these three internal movements, fear, want and freezing?

If you are like most of the countless of our workshop participants, *your answer would be around 80% of your energy.*

This incredibly high share of your energy is literally feeding, sustaining, nurturing, and often unknowingly expanding this projective and virtual alternative reality.

If most of our participants find that around 80% of their energy is literally sequestered by this condition, this would clearly leave us with a mere 20% of our life-force available. No wonder life seems so daunting, stressful, unmanageable, painful, and insurmountable so often.

Coming back to the original question of, What gets then in the way of Zerospace?, the answer in essence is a very deep, completely primordial and highly efficient *projective algorithmic model* with a very clear agenda: *to survive and stay safe, even at the expense of our happiness, sense of adventure, openness, curiosity, alignment, wholeness, integrity, and joy.*

3

The Puppeteer Elephant in The Room

As shared before, we create an alternative virtual reality that makes it extremely difficult for us to live from a space of openness, alignment, wholeness, joy and understanding. Instead, we spend a good chunk of time fending off imaginary ghosts and trying to mend inaccessible and uncomfortable past torments.

When our clients ask us how real this alternative reality is, we often show them one of those YouTube videos where someone is wearing a virtual reality headset. In these videos, people are often bumping into others, crashing through walls, and breaking all kinds of objects around them. In these videos, people are so entranced by the alternative experience through their VR headsets that they are wholly consumed by it. They are often screaming in panic as they "roll down a rollercoaster at full speed" while destroying household items in the outside world trying to fight fire-breathing dragons in the virtual world.

This of course is a dramatization of the projective condition we live in day after day, yet we also say that our actual experience may be substantially closer to this dramatization than what we may think or feel comfortable accepting.

Another very intriguing aspect of this alternative reality we create is that it is **100% build-to-suit.** In other words, your very own algorithmic alternative reality will be made for you and for you alone, with your family dynamics and cultural habits mixed with *your* trauma, emotions and fears, *your* projections, and *your* anticipations, as well as the ones *you inherited* from your specific lineage and environment growing up.

We want to share with you an image that clearly illustrates not only the human condition we are in but also the profound implications that it has. When we talk about the proverbial elephant in the room, we tend to refer to *an uncomfortable situation that is undoubtedly present but avoided because we find it better not to be addressed.*

When we are talking about our projective algorithms and the alternative virtual reality that these mechanisms create, at some deeper level we also highly suspect that there is more to life, and that these projections are mostly unnecessary, untested, unvalidated, and often simply irrational. Another clear sign of this knowing is how we often deeply long to be liberated from these constraints, and the recurrent thought that there must be more to life than this survivalist rat race.

We have a deep intuition pointing to the understanding that these heavy, perceptional layers of existential, unwelcomed add-ons are clearly not part of our essence. We know at some deeper level that these truly confusing and heavy layers of perception should *not* be limiting our full human potential and experience.

The tension and dissonance surrounding this condition is so intense that we try to:
1) Strongly conceal these fears and projections, or
2) Engage in battle with them, or
3) Think we are faulty, not good enough, weak, as we live with very low self-esteem consistently comparing ourselves with others, or
4) Do our best to ignore them and assume they are not there and then numbing our discomfort with food, alcohol, work, drugs, the internet, etc.

Without being fully aware of it, this approach creates and sustains our own existential **elephant in the room**. In this case though, the "room" is not a relationship, or the office, or a political party, but rather, ***it is your own inner world.***

To make things even harder, our inner-world elephant in the room would not only be there, taking tremendous space and consuming 80% of our energy, but in consequence, it would also be *driving* and *determining* 80% of our life's interactions and outcomes. Think of this elephant as a subconscious survival-driven, hyper-clumsy machine with an agenda.

This elephant sees the reality surrounding you very poorly and has considerable trouble moving around life's challenges and opportunities, given its algorithmic tendencies and constraints. So, instead of only being an uncomfortable presence in our inner space, the elephant becomes a Puppet Master that tries to guide us with an additional metaphorical eye patch and a leg crutch. This experience of ourselves includes how we see ourselves, how we present ourselves to others, how we see others, how we see the world, what we expect from the world and how we interact with it.

The Puppeteer Elephant in the Room

If 80% of our drive, our interactions with others, our self-motivation, our self-assessment and our self-esteem, as well as our reactivity, our wants and our disconnection are driven by this algorithmically imposed, projective process that resembles a puppeteer elephant in our inner room with serious mobility and perceptional issues, then the next question that begs addressing is, Who or what am I, *really*? Who is this tied-up, limited, lonely, fearful, doubtful, reactive, incomplete, frozen and absent-minded individual? And even more so, how would I live life if I were to become free?

4

Innocence

It is important to clarify that **there are no guilty parties** in this complex phenomenon. We are all innocent even when considering all the pain and confusion that we inflict on others or that is inflicted on us. It is easy for our mind to go into the common righteous space where we either assume guilt or assign guilt, especially when the slick puppeteer elephant is hiding behind our personal identity.

Quite often – literally – *we do not know what we do*. When this happens, it is easy for others and for us to assign all kinds of untested assumptions and purposes behind our actions and intentions or the actions and intentions of others. By doing this, we naturally become weary of ourselves and others.

There is not much behind this limiting human condition but honest confusion. No mysterious plan or agenda is at work here. The reality is that things are much simpler than what we imagine. In essence, we are often driven to act led by the strings of the elephant with one clear and blinding agenda: *to do what in the moment feels like the best option for our survival and safety.*

Even though we are innocent of being mostly driven by unconscious projective algorithms, we must be careful not to use this to justify harming others and ourselves. On the one hand, we are deeply innocent of this troubling human condition and on the other, **we are the only ones that can actually do something about it.** Hence a profound implication of responsibility as well as innocence arise simultaneously

In other words, we do not know why we do what we do, and at the same time we are the **only ones** that **can** do something about this. We are the only ones responsible for taking care of the pain and being algorithmically referenced and out of alignment.

5
IBC: Dissolving the Algorithm

For our regular everyday minds, it may be easy to think that if we fight the algorithm directly, we will be able to subdue it or eliminate it at some point. We could probably wage several battles against it or even start a great big war as we do for so many other things internally or externally in this world, always with questionable and relative results.

In this case, the more we fight the algorithm, the more we feed its survivalist foundation, and therefore the stronger it gets. It is as if a double-door safe would get molecularly stronger every time we try to blow a hole on it. So, how do we go about resolving this condition to address the algorithm? Well, in our consistent and verified experience, we can do this by practicing IBC.

In essence, IBC is a process in which we go through the following stages:

1) **We identify an algorithm-based issue.** We identify a problematic experience or issue in our lives. We welcome it and allow it to show itself inside. It can be in the form of a thought, an image, an emotion, or a body sensation. We welcome the experience without judging ourselves for feeling what we are feeling.

2) **We shine the light of awareness towards this issue** by reminding ourselves of the five aspects of the Spirit of Inquiry: Am I willing to be wrong? Am I willing to be curious? Vulnerable? Uncomfortable and humble around this issue? If we answer yes, we then move into the IBC questions.

3) **We access a powerful internal space of clarity, understanding, vision, and possibilities** to explore the algorithm that is not allowing us to see clearly. In this way, we access what was previously inaccessible now leading to the source of self-discovery and inner understanding.

4) Having embodied a profound direct realization of the situation that we inquired into, **we now naturally, effortlessly, and joyfully move forward** with deep clarity and understanding of our issue and the clear next steps that would naturally and effortlessly follow.

5) If there is anything still getting in the way of a fully expansive experience of inner freedom and understanding (Zerospace), we then explore this remaining issue and go through the IBC process again (or as many times as needed)

until we finally arrive at a clear and unquestioned experience of Zero.

We will explore the IBC process in more detail including step by step instructions on how to use it in the second section of this book.

It is important to note that resolving an algorithm and fully reaching Zerospace is a powerful experience, yet this unique experience will rarely dissolve our entire algorithmic condition instantly. Algorithms are designed to be breached from time to time and then get back to their original solid state. Algorithms are strong, flexible, predictable, resilient, as any survivalist-driven mechanism should be. That is why to resolve and liberate us from the *entire algorithmic condition* we need to:

1) **Consistently access and recognize Zerospace.** In other words, visit Zerospace often (which has its own immediate and powerful rewards such as a sense of clarity, understanding, expansion, self-reliance, safety, compassion, and love). When in Zerospace, make sure that *you are fully aware that you are there.*

2) ***Relax into the experience of Zerospace.*** *Trying to hold on to it will only make you lose it,* so this point is not about force or attachment, but rather about **relaxing into** Zerospace. You will clearly know the difference between when you are in Zerospace and when you are not. There is no mistake about this.

3) **Expand** and **live** your life from Zerospace. In short, cultivate the space, deepen the experience, and embody it in every cell of your body.

The more time you spend in Zerospace, the less the algorithmic condition is nurtured, and the more it naturally and gently dissolves to the point that it cannot sustain itself anymore.

The full dissolution of the algorithmic condition will deliver you into an unabridged experience of freedom that is extraordinarily radiant and essentially complete.

Zerospace

Zerospace is the absence of internal algorithmic projections, which fully allows your true Self to shine and become completely embodied.

6

Is Your Zero, Their Zero, My Zero?

No. Plain and simple.
And at the same time, yes.
Again, plain, and simple.

My Zero is *not* your Zero in the sense that you would generally not live or describe Zero in the exact same way someone else might. At the same time, my Zero *is* your Zero in that Zero is that same internal space of awareness where we experience ourselves as clear, whole, joyful, aligned, complete, understanding, in peace, and free.

A major complication when we practice IBC arises when we compare our self-inquiry experience or our experience of Zerospace with the experience and process of others. How often do we get to Zero and how often do others do? How intense, sustained, or profound is my experience of Zero when compared to others? How are others describing Zero as opposed to how would I describe Zero?

The bottom line here is that your Zero is *your* Zero. That's it. Your Zero does not need to feel or sound like other Zeros, and at the same time, all is well if it does.

The experience of Zero has different levels, depths, nuances, and moments for each of us, and none of us have access and deep understanding of the Zero experience of others. Each of us, individually, is the only one that can say and know if we are in or out of Zero. You will see how to identify when you are in Zero in the next section of the book.

It is important to underline that in this process of transformation there are no linear or universal benchmarks to assess your level of "advancement" or "development". Your quest to persistently live life from Zerospace is yours, and yours alone. The path can be slow at first and at lightning speed later, or vice versa. One minor insight can deliver profound clarity at times, and at the same time an apparently immense insight can deliver tenuous clarity or even some confusion.

What we do know for sure for ourselves is that far away from structures, steps, levels, benchmarks, supervision, judgement or assumptions about self and others, there is *one* and *only one* thing left to do in this life for us: **to keep accessing, identifying, recognizing, relaxing into, cultivating, returning to, and expanding our Zerospace-led life!**

7

Zero is Zero is Zero

When it comes to Zero, everything that we rationalize, imagine or expect about Zero is a projection, an illusion, a fantasy. In other words, by definition, **Zero cannot be anything we think it is**. At the same time, everything that gets in the way of Zero is a montage, a veil, a distraction, or some form of algorithmic noise that disconnects us from who we really are behind the innocent confusion that we experience almost every day. We often say to our clients and to participants in our programs: **Remember that Zero is so Zero that it cannot even be Zero.**

In other words, Zero is the complete absence of every algorithm. It is only when we reach this zero-algorithm space that our endlessly projecting elephant finally stops and allows for our Being to flow in its full radiance and fill every corner of our existence.

Some clients and participants normally fall into the trap of trying to *imagine* or *project* the experience of Zero without existentially arriving at Zero. In other words, they *project* (imagine or rationalize) an experience of Zero that is not the ***lived experience of Zero***. In these cases, it is common to hear assumptions such as "Zerospace is lonely", or "Zerospace is cold and detached", or "Zerospace is like endlessly falling into nothingness", or "I will lose myself in Zerospace", or "I will lose you if you embody Zerospace" or "My life (or your life) will collapse in Zerospace". Our imagination cannot represent what Zerospace will be from a place of algorithmic tension. We will only get to Zerospace by directly accessing and embodying it.

How can Zerospace be experienced as a falling into nothingness? For something to actually "fall", we first need an "up" and a "down" or a "high" and a "low"; in other words, we need a point of reference. How can you fall when in Zerospace there is nothing to fall from or fall towards? *The lived experience of Zerospace is closer to the experience of full sustainment: an experience where there is nothing lacking or missing. It is an experience of wholeness where our true Being shines.*

Zerospace is the experience of the absence of algorithmic tendencies, allowing for who we truly are to shine through.

8

Responsibility and Zerospace

We have made very clear in the disclaimer of the book that if you engage in any practices shared in this book, you would be doing so under your absolute and untransferable responsibility. All content and practices in this book are presented as an invitation into the exploration of our internal world for the purposes of self-discovery, personal understanding, and most importantly inner freedom. Again, if you have chosen to engage with the content and practices presented in this book, you are doing so at your own risk. The content and practices in this book are not intended for providing advice, diagnosis, prescription, treatment, or cure for any condition, nor do they address any specific situation.

Naturally, individuals remain wholly responsible for their own understanding, experience and actions. Appropriately qualified, licensed or professional support should be sought to address particular needs.

The *most important* thing to know for the IBC practitioner is that *the experience of Zerospace in and of itself is absolutely a non-issue for the experiencer.* **And this is the case at all times.** In other words, *at no point can the experiencer have an issue with Zerospace, given that Zerospace is in essence the purest form of the experiencer.*

This may not be necessarily the case though for those *around* the experiencer, especially if others are particularly used to the experiencer's confused and reactive, algorithmic patterns and count on these to navigate life. In this case, external observers of Zerospace may experience someone else's experience of Zerospace as something that is threatening or obstructing their relationship, or even something that is causing the other person to change in ways that the witness of the experiencer might consider risky or problematic. In this case, it is very important to clarify and understand that the issue is not in and around Zerospace or the experiencer of Zerospace but rather with the projections, apprehensions and assumptions that are being cast onto Zerospace and onto the experience of the Zeronaut.

Also, it is *very important* to know that as a practitioner of IBC, *the only times that Zerospace may be perceived as a problem or an issue is when we are not in actual Zerospace and we are still algorithmically referenced, believing that we are in Zerospace.* Zerospace in and of itself is pure and endlessly spacious; anything other than that appearing to come from Zerospace is another projection of the survivalist algorithm trying to reassert dominance over the liberating inner space.

As we sustain and stabilize the new inner experience of Zerospace, we gain an embodied experience of the present moment. Because of this, you may notice less emphasis in your historical past and potential future, and therefore you may possibly experience or assume that your memory is not working as efficiently as it should. Nevertheless, in these cases as soon as we focus on what we need to retrieve from memory, or plan into the future or act upon, our memory and planning skills appear on demand and maybe even better than before.

Another aspect of Zerospace is that it may naturally open the door to new life adventures or relationships and close the door to others, potentially changing the landscape of our lives sometimes in significant ways. This does not mean that such a change *must* happen to stabilize Zerospace. It is not the case at all for either one way or the other. There is *no* "this is how Zerospace must look like" anywhere, ever in this model.

Zerospace is never a justification to harm or abuse others in any way. Using the concept of Zerospace to deliberately harm others is a manipulation of it and a comeback of the confused algorithmic mind trying to reassert power over you. As stated many times in the book, a *Zerospace-led life is a naturally emergent, compassion-driven, wholly understanding, action-delivering, internally peaceful and boundlessly freed experience of Being.* Any internal experience that cannot be sustained within this rendering of Zerospace is not Zerospace, even if someone is erroneously referring to it as Zerospace. Zerospace provides clarity, true compassion, inner understanding, and self-emergent love as a natural by-product of this internal alignment; therefore, all changes become self-sustaining and natural.

It is quite probable that at some level our survivalist biology will naturally resist the dissolution of projective algorithms, given that they have been mostly pseudo-protective. Therefore, it is relatively normal to experience a moving back and forth between Zerospace and stress, anxiety, or fear. Our survivalist biology may sense that something strangely liberating is going on and try to reassert dominance over *being* by increasing anxiety or fear at times. Yet, because we are not directly fighting or battling the algorithmic structure, we can always come back to Zerospace with our next IBC session. If we persist in the practice of IBC, we will prevail, and at some point we will remain in this extraordinarily unique and profoundly exquisite experience of clarity, compassion, alignment and understanding.

With IBC we can engage in, explore and address absolutely any issue that we can bring our attention to. If we are willing, open, and able to inquire into an algorithmic assumption, the IBC process will be able to guide us through the storm and the depth and then to the clarity, the understanding, the joy and the expansiveness.

You can use IBC with issues you even perceive as coming *from* the IBC method itself or even *from* Zerospace itself. If IBC or Zerospace is apparently doing "this" or "that" to you or having "this" or "that" unwelcomed effect or having "this" or "that" unwelcomed experience, you can always work on it using IBC.

To further clarify, IBC will not work if you are *not willing* to explore deeply who you are. IBC is for those who *are willing* to be open and explore what they think about themselves, the world and others, for those who are willing to recognize, relax into, and live their lives from the space where they can truly be themselves.

III

Inquiry-Based Coaching

~

What if you had a clear, simple, and grounded methodology to reliably and persistently access, recognize, relax into, and live a Zerospace-led life?

~

1

Ease of Transformation

The IBC model, as opposed to many other human development models, is based on the principle of *ease of transformation*. In other words, and as counter intuitive as this may sound to some, when we practice IBC, we change for the better, *effortlessly*. Yes, you can read that line again, or better yet, we will reprint the line here to confirm this is not an editorial error: ***When we practice IBC, we change for the better, effortlessly.***

Forget about the endless pursuit of betterment through sacrifice, will, inner hardship, strategizing, planning, pushing, using blame or shame, pulling and cajoling. Not necessary.

If you were to look back at any of your transformational processes in life that have been driven by sacrifice and force of will, you would clearly see that most (if not all) of them have not worked. You may also clearly see that the ones that have worked continue to demand punishing amounts of energy and dedication from you, with the apparent benefit bordering on misery.

The principle of transformation through sustained effort is one of the algorithms responsible for most of the pain and suffering associated with personal growth in this world and a sure source of disappointment, further discouragement, and even potential depression.

With IBC, we change because it just makes sense. We change because it is effortless, and because it is the natural thing to do next. It would be clearly counterproductive not to change in the face of what we now know, have fully seen, or have clearly realized.

Going deeper still, with IBC *we change because the impediments to change dissolve of their own accord*. The impediments to change dissolve because we deeply realize and have clearly seen for ourselves, and with every cell in our body, that what we were previously doing to ourselves (and others) makes absolutely no sense and is obviously a source of confusion and suffering.

It is certainly like the time when you were a child and burned yourself with a match, stove, candle, or something similar. That is when you clearly just "got it" and simply realized that burning your finger *is not something that works for you.* You did not have to make a great effort to remember that "fire burns" by burning yourself again, and again, and again, ten or twelve times until you actually understood.

Zerospace delivers a kind of deep and transcendental learning and understanding that becomes alive in our awareness and brings about change powerfully and effortlessly. Zerospace produces that deep existential realization where we just *get* that sustaining and supporting the irrational, illusory reality we have innocently created no longer makes sense.

With IBC, we become deeply aware of our wholeness. A wholeness beyond, or behind, or before or underneath the projected world we have assumed to be our reality.

2

Finding Clarity for Yourself

The industry of "advice giving" is alive and thriving in this world. Everyone has some package of advice for you all the time: your media feed, news outlets, magazines, etc. We are constantly bombarded by statements such as "The 5 steps to better relationships", "The 3 principles to success", "The 4 best foods to eat", "The 7 strategies to become rich and keep your money" or "The 9 foods to avoid losing weight".

    We can also find ourselves as recipients of very specific advice (generally what comes from family, friends, close relationships, co-workers, etc.). This advice often sounds like, "You should move from that job", "You should sign up for yoga", "You should leave the relationship", "You should stay and endure whatever it takes", "You shouldn't trust that person", "You should lose weight" or "That person is the only one you can trust".

    The thing with advice, as selfless, compassionate, and supportive as it may be, is that ***advice-taking simply***

does not work. Again, taking advice ***does not work***. And once more, ***it does not work***. There. Clear.

Advice taking does not work, not because others are not dispensing high quality content or because we are openly trying to resist the support we are receiving from others. The problem with advice taking is that as human beings we only achieve true lasting change when ***we internally find and corroborate for ourselves what we need to learn.***

If what we need to learn is externally sourced, we will not be able to bring it in, we will not implement it, and we will not embody it in a lasting and sustained way. If advice-taking worked, we would have solved and settled the human condition already long ago. It is impossible for us to take something that is an intellectual abstraction from someone else and incorporate it within as valid, true, reliable and trustworthy.

It is quite common to see examples of relationships where one individual in the relationship has been recommending, hoping for, or expecting a particular behavioral outcome from their partner and simply never see it happen. Even if at times we seem to perceive some change in the expected behavior, it is mostly short-lived and quite stressful for the individual that is hoping to change.

Let us imagine a relationship where a partner is requesting the other to eat healthy. The requesting partner is frustrated because the non-complying partner simply does not understand or commit to it. At some point in the relationship, the non-complying partner may one day appear completely amazed by the clarity of a particular insight they found about the transcendental merit of healthy eating. After this self-reported earth-shattering insight, one would see the previously non-complying partner actively and successfully eating in a healthy way at every meal wherever they go. No sweat to it!

When the non-complying partner shares their amazing "discovery" with the compliance-expecting partner, the latter may be clearly shocked to see that this apparent amazing discovery was *exactly* the same solution they had been offering the non-compliant partner probably for decades.

Yet, when the compliance-expecting partner says to the non-complying partner: "This is exactly what I have been saying to you all along!", most probably the previously non-complying partner will say something like, "You have never said that before" or "No, this is completely different" even if the recommendation is the same as the discovery. The fact that the recommendation was not alive, clear, seen, and incorporated wholly in the previously non-complying partner made it impossible for them to truly see and engage with it.

Realizing that only what we truly find within and for ourselves is powerful enough to generate change should be a source of tremendous relief.

How much time, energy and personal resources are we investing in this absolutely failed expectation of change through external advice? How long have we been investing our energy, hopes, time, and resources, attempting to fix others? Has it helped yet? Superficially, maybe. Temporarily? Perhaps. Artificially? Yes. Sustainably? Probably not.

3

The Power of Open-Ended Questions

I am neither especially clever nor especially gifted. I am only very, very curious

~ Albert Einstein

Open-ended questions in general allow for a natural process of **wide curiosity** which is the foundation of all discovery, all understanding, and all true realization. They do not have a one-stop-shop answer.

Without open-ended questions, humanity would have never wondered how to fly, how to build immense skyscrapers or how to cure diseases. Open-ended questions are in and of themselves the source of all exponential knowledge and discovery.

Even pre-verbal infants ask by simply pointing to things and fully absorbing the answer. Open-ended questions are the origin and the source of most applied humanist endeavors. In essence, open-ended questions allow for deep pondering and an honest exploration of internal or external evidence.

In IBC we have developed 16 questions that we have divided into 5 main questions and 11 sub-questions to be used in the exploration, transformation, and dissolution of what may impede our direct experience of Zerospace.

These 16 questions are inherently open questions. That is why we always encourage all IBC practitioners to move away from their pre-programmed, algorithm-driven assumptions when answering the questions. In other words, *open-ended questions bring a natural disruption into the usual algorithm-driven mind chatter.* They bring a pause, a waiting, a wondering, a watching. They bring curiosity and space.

Answering open-ended questions starts with silence, openness, and awareness. It does not start with assumptions, or content, or suggestions, or expectations (even if they are quite refined). Answering open-ended questions also does not start with jumping into our internal search engine to access the "approved" or "right" files of internal answers quickly. These answers often carry with them the burden of long held and unquestioned assumptions and projections that may not even be ours, and are quite often even several generations old.

It is also important to clarify that IBC is not about blindly rejecting previous assumptions only because they are a previous assumption. Rather, it is about examining and openly inquiring into the assumptions to see if they get to stay or are ready for an update. If they do get to stay, it is because they have passed the threshold of alignment and consistency that Zerospace kindly and effortlessly demands from us; if they do not, it is because they have not passed that threshold and we have now found new answers that do.

4

Identifying the Issue

In order to practice IBC, we first need to identify an issue that is getting in the way of our best experience of life. In our programs we have basically four kinds of entry points into IBC where we can find issues to bring into the inquiry process: **1)** *obstacles*, **2)** *relationships*, **3)** *the body and* **4)** *identities.*

1) Obstacle Inventory Form. In this form, we first identify an important and relevant goal in our life. After doing so, we identify three sets of potential obstacles to that goal in three different categories:

a) *External Obstacles.* These obstacles are the ones we could seemingly validate or justify referencing our exterior, or what is happening "outside" of us, for example, "He is not considering me for the promotion", "They don't want to change their mind; "They are making cuts without looking at personal impact" or "He has stopped loving me". Any issue that we can apparently validate externally, or that has to do with others and generates discomfort or stress could be used as an external obstacle.

b) ***Internal Obstacles.*** These obstacles are generally obstacles that tend to be self-critical and start with an "I", for example, "I am not good enough", "I don't have what it takes" or "I disappointed them". Any issue that we can validate internally and that has to do with 'me', that generates discomfort or stress and points towards myself could be used as an internal obstacle.

c) ***Big Picture*** **or** ***Universal Obstacles.*** These obstacles are generally obstacles that tend to relate to the larger themes of life and the assumptions we may have around them. They generally start with words like "The World", "Society", "People", "Work", and "Money", for example, "The world is harsh; "Society is unfair" or "Money is difficult to get". Any issue we can validate at the big picture level which generates discomfort or stress could be used as a big picture or universal obstacle.

After finishing our list of obstacles, we choose the one that has the most weight or energy behind and bring it as the ***issue*** to address in the IBC Process.

2) Relationship Reset Form. This form is used as an invitation to think of someone in our life with whom we are experiencing difficulties or stressful times. After we identify the person, we ask ourselves the following five questions, writing short and clear answers to each of them:

a) How is this person affecting me?
For example, "He is criticizing me."

b) What is this person missing?
For example, "He doesn't see that my options are limited".
c) What could this person do differently?
For example, "She could see my point of view", and
d) How should this person show up for me?
For example, "He should be open and supportive of me".

After finishing our list of answers to the questions, we choose the answer that has the most weight, activation, or energy behind it, and we bring it as the *issue* to address in the IBC Process.

3) **Bodily Sensation Form**. In this form we invite the client to identify a tight or stressful sensation in their body even though there may not be any clarity around its meaning, origin or the thoughts that surround it. These sensations may include tension, stress, apprehension, anxiety, worry, resistance, uncertainty, exasperation, doubt, insecurity, or dread. After identifying the sensation in the body, we invite our client to answer the following questions:

a) Where in your body do you experience this sensation? (e.g., neck, head, or stomach)
b) How would you describe the sensation? (e.g., prickling, emptiness, buzzing, pressure, or tension)
c) If this sensation had a color, texture, form, and size, what would these be? (e.g., dark brown, coarse, round, or covering my entire mid-body)

After filling the form, we ask our client to then move to the IBC questions and identify *"This Sensation"* as the *issue* to be explored and continue answering the IBC questions with the sensation present and as the center of the inquiry process.

4) **Identities**. In this approach we do not use a set-up form in the same way we do for the initial three. Rather we use a different frame set and a modification of the IBC questions. In this approach, we use the different identities that arise from us in given different situations, in other words, those "personas" we turn into when we are presented with a particular challenge in life. A detailed explanation of this approach is included further in this book.

These are the four main approaches that we have generally used so far in our training sessions, but these are certainly not the only possibilities. We have seen these four evolve throughout time, and we know they will keep evolving as we keep finding new and more powerful ones. We often also use what we call the **Weather Person** approach. This approach is basically about closing your eyes, moving your attention to the center of your inner system (however that shows up for you) and, as the TV Network Weather Person would do, simply paying attention to what emerges inside your internal system and work on that. To illustrate, "a storm moving in from the south" might be remembering dinner last night with a sibling, "Winds from the north" may be second-guessing yourself around a presentation that you will have next week or "Two inches of snow" might be the apprehension you are feeling about the nagging family member you are not comfortable seeing next week. Many of our students use this approach as part of their daily IBC practice after having investigated the important themes in their lives such as relationships, work, goals, and success. In essence, anything that can be identified as an ***"issue"*** in your life can be brought into IBC and is eventually a door to access Zerospace.

Issues are the actual source for our growth in the IBC model. They are a crucial component of the process. Issues in general invite us to see and directly acknowledge the pre-programmed algorithm that is ticking and hiding as an assumption to be questioned behind the veil of our conditioned identity.

There are absolutely no limitations or barriers to what we can or cannot bring to IBC. This is one of the most powerful aspects of IBC. You can bring a bodily sensation, a judgment of yourself, judgments of others, an obstacle, a sorrow, a complaint, a joy, a hope, love, sadness, a general sense of dread, apprehension, doubt, etc. You can bring one issue, two issues or three issues, or put the whole issue or internal experience into a symbolic blender and work from there. There is absolutely nothing that cannot be brought to and sustained by the light of open, honest inquiry.

5

The IBC Questions

These 16 questions (divided in 5 main questions and 11 sub-questions) were born after years of practicing several models of personal transformation including self-inquiry, contemplation exercises, the highest and most selective forms of Himalayan meditation, intensive shamanic ceremonies, explorations into the realms of formal philosophical academic thought, as well as practices in independent educational leadership and entrepreneurship.

HOW DO WE ACTUALLY PRACTICE IBC

IBC can be practiced individually, facilitated by a coach, in pairs, or in group settings. When practiced individually, our suggestion would be to write down the answers to the questions on paper, in a journal or electronically. The IBC App is also available for both IOS and Android. This app is a great resource to guide you in your own self-inquiry process.

When working in pairs, there should be a client and a facilitator role clarified before starting. The facilitator would then ask the questions and hold the space for the client to go deep in their exploration. Facilitating IBC may seem straight forward, but, it is not that simple. Holding space is very different than having a conversation, gossiping, commiserating together, or trying to fix someone. Holding space is about allowing our client to deeply explore their experience while the facilitator remains as a stable metaphorical raft floating on the expansive seas of inquiry.

When practicing IBC, we offer facilitators 10 key recommendations to best support their clients:

1. **Trust the questions completely.** Don't modify, skip, add or change the order of the questions.

2. **Be a true listener.** Listen with your whole body. This is the best way to support your client's inquiry.

3. **Do not offer advice.** Offering solutions or going into 'fix mode' gets in the way of your client's process.

4. **Trust your client's process.** Remember that what we do not discover for ourselves has no true impact in our lives.

5. **Do not rationalize the process.** Do not anticipate, project, or assume any outcome of the process. Go through it and see.

6. **Facilitations are confidential.** Nothing we hear from our client when we facilitate is ours to share.

7. **Bring your client back when needed.** Our mind naturally wanders and justifies its concerns. This is not IBC. Simply ask the current question again to bring your client back.

8. **Notice your own algorithms.** As you facilitate, identify your own obstacles and projections. Work on them later. Notice and come back to your Zero.

9. **Facilitate from Zerospace.** As often and as deeply as possible, open to curiosity and the mystery of inner exploration. This is not a "figure it out" process.

10. **Seek guidance when needed.**

When facilitating a group, we generally have one person guide the process by having them ask the questions out loud and allowing each participant space and time to write down their answers. This approach can also be used with participants verbalizing their answers (instead of writing them down). Sharing their inner exploration and findings with the group as they answer each question in short, concise sentences is often a very powerful experience for all.

THE IBC QUESTIONS

After identifying the issue and preparing our mindset for the process, we engage in the following questions:

A much more detailed example of how to answer the IBC questions will follow in another chapter of this section

How *valid* is this issue for you on a scale of 1 to 10? (1 = Lowest to 10 = Highest)

1. How do you validate this issue?
a. Describe the thoughts, images, sensations, and emotions that validate this issue.
b. Who do you "turn into" (in your mind) when you validate this issue?
c. Who do others "turn into" (in your mind) when you validate this issue?

2. How do you exaggerate, disconnect, or freeze, when you validate this issue?
a. What is repetitive, cyclical, or pattern-like when you validate this issue?
b. What assumptions are you making about yourself, life, and others when you validate this issue?

3. What are you not able to notice when you validate this issue?
a. Who are you right now without validating this issue?
b. What is now new, fresh, exciting, and clear that was not there before this inquiry?

c. How is this issue an opportunity?

4. What specific and concrete next steps are now clear for you?
a. Would you like to share your next steps with someone else? If so, whom?

5. What is left?
a. How valid is the original issue still after this inquiry?
(0 = Nothing to 10 = Maximum)
b. What issue is remaining behind this number (if not zero)?

THE IBC APP IS AVAILABLE FOR IOS/ANDROID

6

Getting to Zerospace with IBC

As you noticed in the previous IBC questions, at the beginning of every inquiry, we ask our clients to identify how valid is the issue to be explored for them in a scale of 1 to 10? (1 = Low to 10 = Max). This gives us a starting value that we will compare with a later question. If a client starts with a 10, or a 9, or an 8, they may finish the inquiry process with a 3, a 2, a 1 or even with a Zero.

When a client finishes the inquiry process in Zero, they have reached Zerospace.

When they have reached Zerospace, we invite the client to 1) ***recognize*** the space of Zero, 2) ***relax*** into the space of Zero, 3) ***expand*** the space of Zero, and 4) ***remain*** in Zero as a form of meditation for a while, letting their Being know that they have achieved it. ***This is where the recognition, relaxation and expansion happen.***

There is no magic, no spells, no inaccessible theoretical abstractions, or ruminations: simply pure, grounded, honest and to-the-point inner exploration. How do we know we are in Zerospace? We will explore this in detail in one of the following chapters of this section.

If the clients end at a 1, a 2, a 3 or even a 5, the invitation is to identify what remains behind that number, for example "The fear will come back", "I will still fail next time" or "It cannot be this simple". After identifying what remains, we go through the IBC questions again with the remaining issue behind that 1, or 2, or 3 or even 5 and look to take the issue all the way down to Zero. This is the spiral journey we take within until we find our center and alignment.

Inquiry sessions generally run for one hour. In that hour, in our experience, around 60% of clients get to Zero after the first round of questions, while about 80% of clients get to Zero in the second round of questions in that same one-hour session. If our clients have not reached a sustained and clear level of Zero after one hour of inquiry, we generally invite them to keep working on the remaining issue on their own time until they get to Zero or to bring the issue to our next session.

We always invite our clients not to be complacent with a 1, or a 2, or a 3 or even a 5. Even if they do not have time at that moment, we always invite them to continue and go all the way to Zero when they can. Getting to a 1, or a 2, or a 3 or even a 5 may certainly be experienced as an extraordinary success when compared to the 8, 9, or 10 from where they started, yet a 1, or a 2, or a 3 or even 5 pales in comparison with the extraordinary experience of full, unabridged Zerospace.

7

Answering The IBC Questions

We will now briefly go over each of the IBC questions to guide you through them, identifying what is behind each question and how to answer them.

The more we openly, slowly, and deeply we explore each question, the better results we will have. The clearer we are regarding what each question is looking for, the deeper and better results we will have.

Overall, the IBC questions are not answered using our regular, algorithm-driven projective mind. We are not looking for the "right" answer, or for what "I should say" or for what "is adequate". **The IBC questions are emphatically open-ended because we engage with them in full**

curiosity and in full exploration, letting the questions meet a deeper space in our selves.

This Inquiry-Based model of questioning is a form of deep inner exploration rather than only an invitation to build, layer-up or reproduce something that is algorithmically already there and known for us. In other words, when we pose an IBC question, we allow our full internal universe to open. And as we do that, we wait. Yes, we wait and become very, very curious. As we wait, we allow for the algorithm-driven, discursive, and reactive mind that often emerges with survivalist algorithms to subside kindly and gently. As we wait, we are allowing that innocent wave of algorithmic reactivity to pass.

After the natural algorithmic reactivity subsides, we focus on what is deeply there now and as we do so, we describe what emerges for us. We describe what we see inside in all honesty and clarity. What shows up after, beyond, behind or beneath the algorithm is our true source of inner clarity and understanding. The IBC questions are an ideal vehicle to access this clear space of awareness.

As we answer the questions, we allow what shows up to keep showing up, like a tea bag steeped into hot water releasing the tea.

We come back to the question being asked as often as needed, and we allow for multiple and deeper answers to come for the same question until we feel that the question has been addressed completely.

It is important to know that as we practice IBC, we are interested in the clear space behind, after or underneath the noise; this space is our true source of internal knowing and understanding.

When it comes to IBC, our answers are more of a *description of what already exists beyond the reactive mind rather than a construction of something that we are putting together.* It is a description of what is being internally shown to us that is not driven by our algorithms, a description of what is already there, available, instead of what "should" or "shouldn't" be there or be happening.

THE QUESTIONS ANSWERED

The Issue: We have already addressed how to identify an **issue** for IBC in a previous chapter of the book. Please refer to that section if you have any questions before moving forward. For the purposes of this presentation of the questions, we will be using *"I am not good enough"*

It is very important to ponder the **mindset questions** *in full honesty before we start the process.* There is probably a risk of trying to acquiesce and answer yes to all the mindset questions to "comply" with the apparent IBC prerequisite. Nevertheless, if these questions do not generate a wholly honest "yes", then whatever gets in the way of that "yes" becomes the new direction of our inquiry. In other words, if there are any "no's" to any of these questions, then we can ask ourselves what is behind the "no" and identify that issue as the one to use and explore through the IBC process. This "no" will be showing us the resistance that is getting in the way of our exploration. This "no" then becomes a great opening to redirect our inquiry in that direction. And so, here are the Mindset questions again:

Mindset questions:
- Are you willing to be wrong about this issue?
- Are you willing to be genuinely curious about this issue?
- Are you willing to be vulnerable about this issue?
- Are you willing to take responsibility for your assumptions about this issue?

How valid is this issue for you on a scale of 1 to 10? (1 = Lowest to 10 = Highest). For this question, we are simply looking at our own or our client's best and most honest self-assessment. This question is important because it gives us a good idea as to where we are starting and what is the level of energy demand that this issue is having in ourselves or our client at the moment we are bringing it to inquiry. It is also a very powerful question because it gives us the benchmark to later evaluates our progress and our results as we move along our inquiry session. The answer should settle at a specific number, for example an 8.

1. How do you validate this issue? We are often asked about the word "validate" in the IBC context. To clarify what we are looking for with this word, we sometimes offer other examples such as "How do you build-up and make this issue real for you?", "What is your proof?", "How do you create or make a case to make this issue real for you?", "What solidifies this issue for you?" or "How do you substantiate this issue?" In the case of the issue being *"I am not good enough"*, some potential answers to the above questions could be, "Because I don't get recognized by my family", Because I cannot get people interested in what I do" or "Because my parent / sibling / partner is constantly giving me examples of how I'm not good enough".

a. Describe the thoughts, images, sensations, and emotions that validate this issue. This is somewhat like the weather-person approach, but in this case we are doing it once we are already inside the IBC process. What shows up for you internally in terms of thoughts, images, sensations, and emotions when you validate or substantiate this issue? What thoughts, images, sensations, and emotions support or solidify this issue? Some potential answers may include "I see images of myself failing", "I feel a void in the pit of my stomach", "I think of my partner recriminating me" or "I feel angry and resentful with this particular person".

b. Who do you "turn into" (in your mind) when you validate this issue? This is a very powerful question, and we do extraordinary work around it. In essence, what we are looking for with this question is to explore the *role/identity/part that you embody/become* when you are validating this issue. For example, for the issue *"I am not good enough"*, we could hear answers like "I turn into a doormat, a beggar", "into the unwanted one", "into the forgotten one" or "into the irrelevant one". We can look for characters in plays or movies that we know and relate to what we are living. We can come up and name a new character like "fearful Pedro" or "angry Tania". As we ask our clients to think of roles / characters that emerge for them, we then explore how this character / identity / personality / part sees the world and how it actually holds a different set of interests, strategies, agendas, values, hopes and dreams than those of our true self.

c. Who do others "turn into" (in your mind) when you validate this issue? This is also a very powerful question. In essence, what we are looking for here is to explore the role that I project, give, or assign *others* when I am validating my original issue. For example, I can explore who do others turn into in my mind when I "turn into" a doormat, or the unwanted one, or the forgotten one, or the irrelevant one.

In this case, it would be easy to find answers like "Others become judges/punishers", "They turn into the ones that are putting me down", "They turn into the uninterested ones" or "They turn into the blind ones".

We often ask our clients to think of specific individuals that naturally show up when we validate the issue we are exploring, and then also to explore the characters we specifically assign to them when we are validating an issue. For example, for the issue *"I am not good enough",* a parent may show up, or a particular key player in the industry I work in, or the person that rejected my latest proposal. In essence, in this question we explore how these characters / identities / personalities / parts of us interact with the roles we assign ourselves or others and with the issue we are exploring in our IBC session.

2. How do you exaggerate, disconnect, or freeze, when you validate this issue? We love this question because it is a brief and direct summary of the three basic movements of the over-reactive, survivalist-based, algorithm-driven mind. These three internal movements of ego are our clear evidence that we are mostly being driven by the algorithmic mind regarding the issue we are exploring. Exploring these movements with the light of inquiry is truly powerful. Some potential answers for this question when we are exploring the issue *"I am not good enough"* would be "I cannot see my value", "I am petrified to move forward with new possibilities" or "I hide and stop caring about myself and about others".

a. What is repetitive, cyclical, or pattern-like, when you validate this issue? Repetition, patterns, and inner cycles are all key tools used by the algorithm-driven mind to support and further sustain the algorithm itself. The actual algorithm is fueled and strengthened by these patterns and by the constant subconscious repetition of the survivalist message. This is the only way it can basically sustain a *false*, a *virtual*, an *artificial* experience of reality. ***In other words, it needs to hold as true something that is not, and to do that it requires a tremendous amount of energy as well as a very convincing and repetitive approach.***

The algorithm is inherently such an unsustainable form of energy in and of itself that it needs to spin around many times to present itself as solid, real, and even menacing. With this question, we can see the illusion for what it is. We also get to notice the "inner pattern machine" in and of itself weaving the dream right in front of our eyes.

There is nothing more disappointing to an illusionist than someone who is really paying attention to every sleight of hand in the show. Some potential answers for this question when we are exploring the issue *"I am not good enough"* could be "I avoid showing up or taking risks", "I constantly feel this void in the pit of my stomach" or "I feel I will never get rid of the dread. It will come back again and again".

b. What assumptions are you making about yourself, life, and others when you validate this issue? At this point in the inquiry, it will be easy for us to see how it is that we are at many levels solidifying this issue through our own projection or anticipation of the issue or around the issue. Also, it is a great opportunity to take responsibility of our own innocent projection of this same issue *towards others*. In other words, how do we sell, market, or promote this version of our virtual reality to others hoping to enlist them to sustain this and to become defenders and promoters of our assumptions, projections, and apprehensions? How do we make this issue real for others so that they can help us validate the issue as true for everyone around us, or at least for as many people as possible, or for the people that most matter in this case?

Some potential answers for this question when we are exploring the issue *"I am not good enough"* would be "I assume my work is not important", "I project they will not approve of what I'm doing", "I project all my past failures to this situation", "I assume life is difficult", "I assume the world is cut-throat competitive" or "I assume life is all suffering".

3. What are you not able to notice when you validate this issue? *And this is where the magic happens.* This is where the internal alchemical transmutation takes us from confusion, apprehension and projection into clarity, understanding, peace, connection, alignment, and insight.

What do you miss when you are *sequestered* by the assumptions, projections, anticipations, and confusion brewing up inside? What are you not able to see? To notice? To appreciate that is already there, available, clear, and open to you? What are you not able to perceive when you are being driven by the validation of the issue you are holding?

*To answer this question,
we take a deep breath,
close our eyes, and
ponder it openly
and deeply*

. . .

*Then, we wait.
And we get curious,
and we wait, and we see inside
again, until insight arises
by itself.*

This is a particular step in the process where we specially invite our clients to wait, relax into the open-ended question, simply zoom out of the limited image we have in the mind and wait for insight. We generally introduce this question with the following preamble when facilitating our clients: *"I invite you to close your eyes now, take a deep breath, and ponder the following question without trying to answer it. Just ponder the question and wait for insight... What are you not able to see or notice? What do you miss when you validate this issue?"*

IBC in general, and this question in particular are invitations into deep exploration. IBC is a form of "guided inner meditation" with the very important difference that in IBC we are not visualizing a beautiful landscape, or white light, or some kind of positive/better outcome, but rather we are fully opening up to the questions as we remain **present, open, and patient** in order for insight to arise **naturally** and **effortlessly**.

> What we see quite often as a result of pondering this question is a form of pure and distilled insight into our own possibilities and potential.

Some potential answers for this question when we are exploring the issue *"I am not good enough"* would be "I can't see that my partner is supporting me now and has always supported me", "I can't see that I have a successful business with great potential as it is", "I can't see that I do have this friend, and that friend, and that other friend, that look forward to connecting with me often" or "I can really see that I am who I am and that is absolutely perfect for me". These are just sample answers amongst many others.

a. Who are you right now without validating this issue? After *seeing* what we are *missing*, after actually *noticing* what we were *not able to see* while driven by the algorithmic mind and the master puppeteer, life and its possibilities substantially open up.

This question invites us to explore this new opening and the new possibilities arising from it now, in the present moment. It invites us to really see the potential and to see ourselves in our lives here and now, living without validating the issue we are addressing with IBC. ***In this question, freedom naturally arises out of clear and self-evident insight.*** Some potential answers for this question when we are exploring the issue *"I am not good enough"* would be "I now live open, clear, and fully available to each moment", "I live curiously and inquisitively asking more questions and making no assumptions", "I live paying attention to what I do have rather than what I don't" or "I am grateful for the experiences and opportunities I do have."

b. What is now new, fresh, exciting, and clear that was not there before this inquiry? *This question is powerful.* It serves as a point in the IBC process where we take stock of our realizations and discoveries so far in only one particular session. Generally speaking, IBC sessions are around one hour long, and it is of amazing value to look at the harvest of each one of those sessions. With this question, we can take stock of what we have seen, of what is now available to us, of what is now self-evident that was not there before, and of what has now arisen from the ashes of confusion and projection and is now a new experience of clarity and potential that was not there before the inquiry. We feel and experience the rise of our own internal phoenix. This question allows you, as well as your client, to see the growth, the reset, the clarity, the understanding, and the result of spending 45 or 60 minutes in one IBC session.

c. How is this issue actually an opportunity? This question points to the completion of the transformation process. We start by having a stressful, projective, energy-consuming, algorithm-driven "issue". Then we run this issue through IBC, transforming it into an open, clear, self-emerging and powerful opportunity. Can you imagine the power and potential that would come into your life from consistently transforming algorithm-driven issues into open, clear, and joyful opportunities at this level of depth and understanding?

Some potential answers for this question when we are exploring the issue *"I am not good enough"* would be "The pain of not feeling good enough brings me back to my IBC practice", "The pain of not feeling good enough is an opportunity to reassess my self-goals and the expectations I have of others" or "It invites me to be more curious and ask more questions".

4. What specific and concrete next steps are now clear for you? In essence, this question opens the door to a very clear, grounded, and useful space of planning and engagement. If you are not a to-do list enthusiast, please do not worry; this question is still for you! The answer to this question can also be "none", "just to notice", "just to breathe" or "to let go and not make any plans". In other words, clarity and liberation show up in many ways and have many different names. Enjoy the spaciousness and possibilities!

It is crucial at this point to remind ourselves that in IBC we do not promote change by pushing or forcing anything within our system. So, the most important aspect of this question is that whatever shows up as next steps for you, these need to be *completely in flow of what is currently self-evident as a result of the insights and inner discoveries we have made as part of the IBC process.* Effortlessness is a crucial component of this form of transformation. Pushing or cajoling ourselves into becoming better is not only completely unnecessary but also wholly counterproductive.

a. Would you like to share your next steps with someone else? If so, whom? Often our discoveries are an amazing source of inspiration and encouragement for ourselves and for others. If we are seeing lasting transformational results, it is easy to understand that we would like to share them with others, and it is also easy to understand that others may be interested in hearing about them. Also, as we allow ourselves to share our next steps with others, we add a layer of accountability to our own personal transformation where we can now count on someone else to support us.

Another perfectly adequate answer to this question is "no" and "no one". Some of the transformational processes we will go through while practicing IBC may very well be for yourself only. There is a powerful form of awareness that arises sometimes when we keep our discoveries to ourselves and hold them clear of any interaction with others' algorithms. The idea here is to respect the internal process, the sensitivity, the vulnerability and also the internal "cooking" or "simmering" or "steeping" of a particular discovery or insight within us for as long as it is needed.

5. What is left? This is an invitation to look back inside and see if there is still any residual or remaining experience of reactivity, anxiety, apprehension, or doubt that was not entirely resolved with the IBC process so far. Our suggestion and our invitation are always to take whatever remains back again through the IBC questions until there is absolutely no reactivity, anxiety, apprehension, or doubt left, in other words until you are at a clear Zero.

a. How valid is the original issue still after this inquiry? (0 = Nothing to 10 = Maximum) *This is the question from which we derived the concept and the expression of Zerospace.* With this question we test the effectiveness of our inquiry session as well as our potential presence within what we call ***the space of zero***, or as we have referred to it many times so far in this book, ***Zerospace***.

When we answer "zero" to this question, our body is centered and at ease, with our breath and eyes relaxed. The mind is empty of reactivity, projections, anticipation, fear, stress, or worry. In this space we also experience a sense of being grounded, aligned, in peace, understanding and with a naturally emerging experience of compassion and love that effortlessly moves us into clear action and grounded purpose.

b. What issue is remaining behind this number (If not zero)? In this question, we look for any specific residual issues that are still getting in the way of our clean and direct experience of the **Zero**. At this point, honesty is paramount. We also need to embrace a true willingness not to let any remaining 1, or 2, or 3, or 5 or 0.0001 to stay unexplored. As we have said before, going from 8 to 3 could very well be a great source of relief and could provide ample understanding and clarity around a particular situation; nevertheless, we often say to our clients that for us a 1, a 2, a 3, or a 5 might very well be a 10 again. Even a 0.00023 is not ok for us compared with the fully unabridged experience of freedom that comes from completely abiding in Zerospace. As time goes by and we move deeper into the practice of IBC, many of us notice an inability to compromise staying in lower numbers at any level when compared with the full experience of Zero. As we recognize, revisit, relax into, embody, and "accumulate" Zerospace, our lives become extensions of this Space. In other words, we begin to live life consistently from Zerospace rather than from the infinitely problematic algorithm-driven mind.

THE PROCESS

At this point we have made a detailed exploration of every question in the IBC model, identifying the potential merits and power of each question. However, it is very important for us to say that the questions work *when they are engaged in the order they are presented,* with none of them omitted

We often say to IBC practitioners that there is no **Zerospace** without Question 4, that there is no Question 4 without Question 3, that there is no Question 3 without Question 2, that there is no Question 2 without Question 1, and that there is no Question 1 without an **issue** to bring to inquiry. In essence, the IBC process is a spiral movement inward that starts with big, broad open-ended questions and ends in the infinite center of the spiral.

It is important for us to share that the practice of IBC generally requires a particularly conducive setting, one of introspection, honesty, and contemplation. We need to give ourselves time to practice IBC in the same way we give ourselves a space, time, and a setting to go to the gym or to produce high-quality work. If you attempt to run through the IBC questions while rushing out of the house, jumping behind the driver's seat of a car, cooking a meal, or dealing with emails, ***it simply will not work***. The reactive, algorithm-driven master puppeteer mind needs to step back for us to be able to engage in inquiry, and this is something that does not happen while we are on the move or in the middle of our everyday, chore-driven life.

As we present this IBC process in detail, it may appear somewhat detailed or complex. It is very important for us to clarify that *with practice, this apparent complexity becomes an absolute non-issue.* As we integrate the questions and become familiar with them, they begin to live within us.

Going through the questions, accessing clarity, and living from that clarity become a fully sustainable and effortless integration.

THE IBC APP IS AVAILABLE FOR IOS/ANDROID

8

IBC and Parts

Very early on in our exploration of this model, we noticed a very interesting and powerful phenomenon. It is now clear to us that the algorithms we have discussed previously at length are not only deeply embodied within ourselves but seemingly very sophisticated internal structures, resembling full, distinct, and independent identities, sub-personalities or parts of ourselves.

In the book Curflexion published almost 10 years ago, I originally called these identities "skippers" and referred to how these skippers appear to be completely independent inner "selves", which are fully autonomous inner beings with their own set of hopes, dreams, personalities, values, and agendas.

In addition to appearing as fully independent inner beings, these identities seem to be triggered or activated given the algorithms that they appear to carry innocently because of early life trauma or existential assumptions eventually solidified throughout our lives and often extremely difficult to heal or change.

I called them skippers particularly because when these identities or parts of us get triggered or activated, they quite literally appear to "take over" our seat of consciousness and completely steer the vessel of our being in the direction that they believe is the best for our system from their innocent yet contrived algorithmic perspectives. As this takeover happens, and as we have seen before, our access and connection to Zerospace becomes seriously compromised.

When these parts of us take over our system or blend with our seat of consciousness, we **are forced** to see the world, life, and others through "their" eyes, emotions, limited resources, incomplete perspectives, and skewed values. This is why, as human beings, we often tend to do things that may be extreme, wholly uncharacteristic of us, or against our best judgement or values. When this happens we generally refer to it as being "blended" with a particular part of us.

Thankfully IBC has demonstrated to be an incredibly powerful method to address this condition as well and be able to generate the space needed from these parts of us when they are triggered or when they are taking over our seat of consciousness so that we may reclaim our Zerospace.

To use IBC for these purposes, the first thing we need to do is to **identify the *part of us* that is triggered as well as the issue that is triggering it.** For example, we can locate an activated part in our bodies where the tension is being felt (e.g., my stomach or my lower back). We can also refer to this as "the part of me that is worried about this or that", or "the anxious Pedro" or "the anticipating Tania". In some other cases, we can even ask the part that is activated to self-identify (for example, by asking directly, "Who are you and what is your issue?")

After identifying the part and its issue, we can then follow the IBC process with the following modifications:

1. On a scale of 1 to 10, how activated is this part of you?
a. Describe the thoughts, images, sensations, and emotions that arise *when you are blended with this part?*
b. Who do you "turn into" (in your mind) *when you are blended with this part?*
c. Who do others "turn into" (in your mind) *when you are blended with this part?*

2. How do you exaggerate, disconnect, or freeze, *when you are blended with this part?*
a. What is repetitive, cyclical, or pattern-like *when you are blended with this part?*
b. What assumptions do you make about yourself, life, and others *when you are blended with this part?*

3. What are you not able to notice *when you are blended with this part?*
a. Who are you *when you are **not** blended with this part?*
b. What is now new, fresh, exciting, and clear that was not there before this inquiry?

4. What specific and concrete next steps are now clear for you?
a. Would you like to share your next steps with someone else? If so, whom?

5. What is left?
a. How activated is this part still after this inquiry?

(0 = Nothing to 10 = Maximum)
b. What issue is remaining behind this number?
(And again, if not zero, you can start the process again until you reach Zerospace.)

Generally this allowance of space develops tremendous clarity and insight for these parts of us to integrate fully back into Zerospace and transform themselves into powerful supportive internal forces. In other cases, though, when the algorithms are too rigid or stagnant, we additionally offer our clients other powerful exercises designed to get to know these parts better and to go deeper into the healing and space-allowing process. To learn more about this approach to IBC, please get in touch with us or visit **innerland.com**

9

IBC and The Spiral

Our good friend and colleague, Markus Tauchmann, who has been leading the Innerland Institute Europe, described to us his experience of IBC as a *"spiraling process into Zero"*.

We often use the image of an Archimedean Spiral to represent IBC. Also since the founding of the Innerland Institute, the logo has always had a Triskelion, a Celtic symbol that includes three spirals representing eternal reconnection to Source and the three elements of deep transformation: 1) the method, 2) the goal and 3) the community of practitioners.

In the spiral shown below, we start with the IBC questions as if we were moving through the more spacious and longer curves on the outskirts of the spiral. As we further engage with the questions and sub-questions, we begin moving inwards into the center spiral until we arrive at the absolute heart of it.

The heart of the spiral is our actual quintessential home, or in other words, Zerospace. Here, we are at the heart of everything; we are where there are no more algorithms to inquire into or dissolve, a space where displacement and movement are not necessary, where we are fully contained. Within this space, we are naturally safe and wholeheartedly at ease.

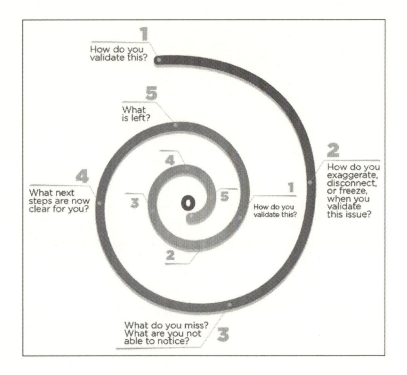

The Spiral into Zerospace

10

How do You Know When You Are in Zero?

This question is actually a *very* simple one to answer. When you are in Zerospace, there is *no single doubt you are in it*. There is a certainty that rings true at every level of your mind and body, and a knowing that is beyond the algorithm-driven mind. There is a form of grounding and alignment in your body and your expressions that is noticeable by yourself and often by others. There is a sense of trust and presence that is unmistakably yours. There is a humble joy that knows everything will be fine, and that we are all in this adventure together.

> Zerospace is an experience that cannot be manipulated through the algorithm-driven mind.

Zerospace cannot be built through will or constructed by positive thinking.

Zerospace is, in essence, the absence of all reactive algorithms. By definition, *Zerospace cannot be created; it can only be uncovered.* This means that *Zerospace is already within* each of us in full splendor. Our issue is that we cannot see / access Zerospace because of the countless and apparently endless distractions fed to us by the algorithm-driven mind. Rather than having to build it or construct Zerospace altogether, we can fully embody it by cleaning up the internal algorithmic noise that gets in the way of Zerospace.

Not only will you be able to know when you are deeply experiencing Zerospace when you practice IBC, but you will also be able to know when you are not there anymore, when you have lost Zerospace. You will know when it is time to go back into your practice. You will start noticing the difference more and more when you are in or out of it, as well as a clear, natural, honest, and self-emerging interest in spending as much time as possible in that extraordinary space.

11

I Will Never Get to Zero

This is a common theme that we notice when we are initially working with some clients. There are basically two possible reasons for this: first, the projective algorithm has deeply convinced them that Zerospace is a myth, and that if not an actual myth, it is extremely difficult to access and stabilize; second, living from Zerospace is such an extraordinarily rare and unique possibility that we are not worthy of accessing it or living from it.

We need to strongly and wholeheartedly sustain that *nothing can be further from the truth*. First, it would of course be relatively common for the reactive and projective algorithm to doubt the existence of Zerospace. This is to be fully expected, and for a very simple reason: the reactive / projective algorithm would need to let go of the hegemonic model of control it maintains over our being to allow for the direct experience of Zerospace. This is something that the algorithm is inherently designed *not* to be able to do, as we have already discussed previously in this book. Hence the importance of kindly and gently circumventing this process by using IBC to reach, recognize, relax into, and expand this extraordinary experience of Being without falling in the trap of the algorithm. With the practice of IBC, we have a very simple and efficient way of getting to Zero.

Access to Zero is only a few rounds of questions (or in many cases, only one single round) away from us at every single moment of the day. The problem is not really the tool itself or the factuality of the existence of Zerospace, but rather the deeper and more problematic issues which arise through our own sense of worth, our own expectation of potential success or our simple inability to provide ourselves the time and space to do so. Practicing IBC will support us greatly in healing this limitation as well.

We hear from our clients quite often that what severely hinders their freedom is assumptions like "I am not worth it", "I have not put in all the work that I need", "I need to address many issues before I can get there", "It cannot be that easy", "It's impossible to reach", "I can access Zerospace momentarily but it will always be impossible for me to sustain it", "It will always disappear and it will never last", "There will always be another issue coming up and getting in the way for me" or "This is an endless process, it will never end". At this point it will be easy for you to see how all these issues are part of the same projective algorithm model getting in the way of our freedom. So, let us be absolutely and completely clear here. ***Zerospace is fully accessible by most people who are open to it***.

In our practice, around 98% of our clients consistently access Zerospace.

In our honest evaluation, the remaining 2% may still be simply in the process of fully opening to it. In essence, Zerospace is not only fully accessible but also fully recognizable and fully sustainable. We clearly know that Zerospace is not a myth because countless participants in our programs consistently and independently attest to its validity and existence. Zerospace is our absolute birthright and from our perspective the apex of human experience.

*You are absolutely,
one hundred percent
worthy of it.*

12

Depth, Honesty, and Consistency

For our IBC experience to be as successful as possible, we need to address three very basic elements: 1) depth, 2) honesty and 3) consistency.

Depth - The IBC questions are not your regular "How are you?" or "What day is it?" type of questions. They are not "should" or "shouldn't" questions, either. They are also different from questions like "What do you want to do when you grow up?", " What are your goals?", "What do you want to strive for?" or "What are you most looking forward to in life?". All these are strategy-inspired, reactive-mind, algorithm-driven, master puppeteer kind of questions. The answers to these questions are either auto-pilot answers or mostly pre-scripted ones. On the contrary, and as we have shared before, The IBC questions are deep, open-ended questions that require time, attention, and contemplation.

We must say that if you are looking for a quick fix to your suffering human condition, you are in the right place. This is because after 20 years of exploration, we have not found anything as efficient as the IBC method to address our inner alienation and suffering. Nevertheless, as much as it is still the most efficient methodology we have encountered, it cannot be considered as magical or fully automatic.

Honesty - It is very important for us to stress that in the practice of IBC there is no competition whatsoever and no need to save face with anyone at all. In this model of transformation, there is no need for hiding or pretending. *All hiding only hinders the one that is hiding.* Our recognition of Zerospace, our ability to relax into it, and our ability to expand it and live from it cannot be faked; this cannot be simulated. You, and only you, are the one that can assess your experience for yourself. You are the only one that can recognize Zerospace. You are the only one that can relax into it, and you are the only one that can expand this space and live from it. If the radiant space of Zero has not introduced itself to you yet, be patient, keep your practice alive and remember that you will absolutely know beyond any doubt when you get there. In our experience, there is no other more worthwhile endeavor in this life. Is there really anything else we would rather do?

Consistency – Our old friend, the confusion-filled, reactive, algorithm-driven mind has many years (or dare we even say millennia evolutionarily speaking) of push, momentum, drive, and synergy behind it. There is such a force and speed to it that it makes it difficult for many of us to even recognize it as the actual source of our primordial confusion and pain. To address this difficult human condition, it would of course be fantastic if we could simply find the switch and turn it off. Nevertheless, as we have seen before, nature is *really invested* in the benefits of the foundational fight-or-flight response, and its potential deviations are of less concern to it. The bottom line is that there is no off switch, and the only way to dissolve this projective algorithm is through a sincere and wholehearted practice in which we slowly and consistently dissolve the foundational blocks that give rise to our confusion, inner confinement, and pain. Simply stated, *without consistency and practice, there is no sustained experience of Zerospace.*

13

Zero-Expansion

Zero-Expansion is the experience of internally "expanding and sustaining" the Zerospace experience to keep reliably moving forward in the process of dissolving the projective algorithm and being able to consistently live from Zerospace.

It may serve to imagine Zerospace as an extraordinary nectar of clarity, alignment, compassion, and love. Would you not want to abide in it as much as you can? If Zerospace were this extraordinary nectar that is gently and naturally able to dissolve the confusion-driven, reactive, and algorithm-driven mind in its entirety, would you not want more of it? If it were a kind of nectar that could also be held in some sort of internal container, would you not save some? Well, if this were the case, then our only to-do job in life's entire to-do list would be to identify, recognize, cultivate, and expand this extraordinary substance.

Yet, how much nectar would we need to sustain and expand so we could fully transcend suffering? Well, the answer would clearly be enough to end up fully dissolving the confusion-driven, reactive algorithm, in other words, enough to dissolve our driving, false alternative reality, allowing us to take off the VR goggles fully and irrevocably.

We may also be interested in finding moments of clarity and understanding where we can just momentarily rest, take a breath, or simply stay there as much as we can. This would be perfectly fine, of course. It is also perfectly fine to aim at using IBC to effectively alleviate your experience of the human condition and to clear up the algorithm only when it becomes too much. In other words, we can be content to practice only when needed, hoping to better navigate confusion and pain. This is perfectly fine. We are all welcome here!

At the same time, know that if you want the full unabridged experience, if you want to go all the way, if this is it for you and there is nothing else you would rather do with your life, you can certainly aim for that, too. From our perspective, If IBC can directly and genuinely alleviate even one instant of confusion and pain for a single practitioner in the world, the effort has been worthwhile. Surprisingly enough, it is our experience that as of today it has deeply and sustainably helped countless participants and already delivered profound and sustainable transformation in many organizations.

14

Living from Zero

"And then one day, pain just stopped. For good. Not a trace of it was left. No inner confusion in sight. Internal radiance replaced doubt, fear, and apprehension. It was all new, and at the same time, this brilliance had been there all along, just underneath it all. This space was boundless and at the same time it felt fully contained and entirely sustained by an infinitely nurturing universe which had no beginning and no end.

A profound understanding of our human condition released prior assumptions of constriction and inner displacement. Love seemed to be our inherent natural condition. Compassion, not as effort but as a freely emerging sense of connection and understanding that just "got" others, "got" where they were coming from, as well as "got" oneself and "got" where oneself was coming from. This is love, not as a fantasy-driven, joy-seeking illusion but as a deeply silent, wholly reliable, and integrally grounded experience preceding all forms of sustainment: an experience of no separation between oneself and others.

Movement as well as purposeful and clear action seemed to arise from a space that exists prior to awareness itself, as if our lives were being driven instead of us being the drivers. And driven not by a careless and inattentive guide but by an exquisite intelligence that sustains and transcends everything. In this space, the questions, What to do?, How to do it? or When to do it? are all fully resolved. The expectations, How to live?, What to say? and To whom? are all settled.

~ *IBC Practitioner*

IV

Practicing IBC

~

What if you could find and access a community of like-minded practitioners supporting each other in the process of identifying, relaxing into, expanding and living from Zerospace?

~

Eight Examples from 10 to Zero

We considered important to include a few detailed examples of actual sessions that have been truly transformational and powerful for our clients practicing IBC. All transcripts included in this section are from actual sessions with clients who have started an IBC process on a 9 or a 10 in terms of level of intensity, activation or validation of the issue ***and have finished the facilitation in complete Zerospace.***

We invite you to allow yourself to fully travel with each clients' experience and find how their path can deeply relate to your own personal experience. When you read through the transcripts, we invite you to go into a contemplative space and take time to deeply consider both the questions and the answers for each of the participants. Join them in their experience of exploration and discovery and do not be surprised if their Zerospace becomes a door to yours as well.

1
I Need Something from the Outside World to Be Complete

Pedro: Violet, what would you like to look into and explore today?

Violet: I would like to say something before we start. My brother died two or three weeks ago. After his death I went to this one-week Innerland retreat with Tania and Markus in Switzerland. It was really powerful and intense. What I realized is that the core assumption of my life is ***I need something from the world and others in order to be complete. I need something from outside to survive and to thrive.***

In my professional life, I think that I need emotional security to really perform. It's well hidden. I'm a very insecure person. I do function very well in the world, but I see that in my professional life I need emotional stability. I need appreciation. I need cooperation. I need a certain amount of harmony. In my private life I need love and appreciation from certain people.

Pedro: And how valid is that you need something from the outside on a scale of 1 to 10?

Violet: This is a 9.

Pedro: And how do you validate that you need something from outside, Violet? What is your evidence? How is it that you are sure that this is the case?

Violet: When I am deprived of the needs that I have mentioned, my mind gets obsessed. So it is no longer possible to be at peace with myself, to be at home with myself. It seems that my mind strives and becomes completely focused on the thing I need, on the thing that I think is absolutely necessary. And it's very torturing to observe and to experience that. I have the feeling that I need this and I need that, my inner freedom is completely lost.

Pedro: I see.

Violet: It is as if I sent myself into exile and as if I were completely lost in a world that cannot or does not want to deliver what I want or what I need. I realized that in all the sectors of my life, this pattern is very active, and it is also very well-hidden because I have built up an identity of a very autonomous woman who thinks clearly and confidently strives for her things. Now I have discovered that this is probably the core reason for my suffering.

Pedro: And what is the experience in your body when you are validating that you need something from the outside and you are not getting it?

Violet: I can experience a body sensation in the area of my heart. The heart gets very unstable, fluttery, a nervous energy, a form of fear. I experience fear in my chest and a hole in the stomach or even lower. I experience a void in the belly and a void in my brain, in my head. It's an uncomfortable feeling, body sensation. I am no longer at home. This is an inner space that has a lot of holes and it's really here, here, in the belly. Yes.

Pedro: Who do you turn into in your mind, Violet, when you are validating that you need something from the outside and you are experiencing these sensations in your body? Just notice, who do you turn into in your mind? Who do you become? What kind of character? What kind of role do you play?

Violet: I become an anxious and a needy person who tries to cover it up, but also a person who is in stress and who is embarrassed to be in this position, a needy person. In a certain way, I turn into a needy child who is afraid that the protection it needs is not delivered, yeah. And I tried to cover it up and I'm sure people feel it around me, a certain amount of insecurity and a certain discomfort, yeah. I am not authentic in this role I give myself.

Pedro: And when you turn into that person or you are playing that role, who do others turn into in your mind when you are validating that you need something from the outside?

Violet: They become mighty people who decide whether to give to me what I need, or not to give it, or perhaps do not want to give it or are not able to give it. They become dangerous people and I, to a certain extent, depend on them. So they get dangerous and mighty. Yeah, Powerful people that are dangerous. They can attack me or appease me, and I am in a position of indignity. I'm no longer at the level of two equals and everybody is not at home within himself or herself, yeah.

Pedro: And when you are validating this issue that you need something from the outside, how do you exaggerate or disconnect or freeze?

Violet: I exaggerate by ignoring that I am interconnected with everyone, ignoring that I'm part of, that I am connected with everyone, and everybody is connected with me, and that in reality, the separation I fear so strongly does not exist, and that it is not in anyone's power to give you something or to deprive you of something, but that life itself serves us by this interconnection that I've mentioned. I exaggerate because I'm in need, but I'm also a powerful human being that is able to give, who is rich. I exaggerate by not acknowledging my inner richness, yeah. And I exaggerate by not understanding that other people have the same needs and desires and insecurities that I have. So I put the other person on a pedestal or in a position of power that in reality does not exist. I freeze when I believe that the other person will or will not give me the thing that I desire. Both situations, both options, whether I get it or do not get it, make me freeze because I lose my dignity, because it's not true. It's a lie. Exaggerate, freeze, and what is the third dimension? Freeze, exaggerate and what else?

Pedro: Disconnect.

Violet: Oh yeah! I completely disconnect from myself, and I disconnect completely from the other person because I make myself to be the object of the other. I lose contact with my dignity, my alignment, that I am a subject, not an object. I do it with the other also because the other turns into a person who either gives me something or does not give me something. So, I objectify the other person, which is also an act of disconnection in itself.

Pedro: And what is repetitive? What is cyclical? What patterns can you see when you are validating that you need something from the outside to function to survive?

Violet: The pattern is to see myself as a person that is not whole, that lacks something essential that needs to be added from the outside. The pattern is not to realize, not to experience fully, and not to embody the experience that I am whole. This is the pattern where I consider myself as separate from the other and separate from the whole; especially the second aspect is crucial in this context because it is really difficult when I am in this inner space. When I enter the space of this pattern, I am no longer able to experience the connectedness, the connection to life itself, to deeply know... So fear arises. It's really fear of death, deep fear of death and not so much on the physical level, but very, very strongly on the psychological, emotional level. This is the death that I fear because I do not fear... I say it easily, but I really think it's true. Emotional death is what I really fear in the form of entering this pattern where I experience others and also probably myself as being in lack, constantly in lack. I need to protect myself and I need allies that I can persuade or seduce to protect myself, this is really the pattern.

Pedro: And what assumptions are you making that sustain or feed this issue?

Violet: Yes, I create these assumptions, by this idea that the worth that I have is delivered by or is attributed to others. By accusing others when they do not give me what I want, by manipulating them. The main strategy is by controlling, by controlling situations and by anticipating situations very strongly. In my professional practice, I make concepts on how to do things, I've always thought, oh, I'm conceptually very strong, but now I realize that this is not really the case. So, for example, in private, in personal relationships, it can look like this, that I negotiate. I ask, What is the frame? What is important? What is our vision? It's very subtle, very subtle, but it is a form of manipulation. It is an intellectual style of manipulation, and I see that.

Pedro: Violet, let me invite you to close your eyes now and take a deep breath. And ponder the following question without trying to answer it. Just ponder the question and wait for insight. When you are validating that you need something from the outside, what are you missing? What are you not able to see? What is already there for you that you cannot access because you are validating this issue? And just stay there and wait to be shown.

Violet: [After a long pause] That there is no outside; that the outside is just a projection of my mind. It is just an imaginary dialogue with me. There are no others to give me something. It's not a danger but rather an invitation to experience that all is in one, in me. And I miss on a very factual level to realize what I have. I have a roof over my head. I have... I can eat. I have heating. My rooms are warm in winter. I have a family. I have friends. I have everything that you can have in this world, and really not to be grateful for that?

I miss that all needs that can be fulfilled by others are so limited, and that they will never fulfill me. I miss that fulfillment of my needs lies within me. I miss being aware that I resist this truth with every cell of my body. The truth that when I'm confused, when I think I'm alone, I assume as a fact that the only way to complete myself is by getting what I need from others. To me this means complete loneliness and being lost in a dark space for all eternity. It's a hellish image that fuels this thought pattern. Yeah. I know that this is not the case. I miss that this is absolutely not true.

Pedro: So how would you live now without validating that you need something from the outside? How would your life be different without validating this narrative?

Violet: I would be very happy, very happy. I would be connected with myself. I would be connected with other people. I would have a lot to give. I would laugh a lot. And I would enjoy having experiences in this world in a playful way, completely indifferent to whether I do them alone or with others, completely indifferent. I would live like, oh, there is someone with me. Let's do this together. Or oh, the other person is gone. Wow, I sustain this wonderful experience within myself. Somehow there is no difference between being alone or with someone else. It's just another kind of setting and it's only good or bad so long as we assume it is one or the other. So, I would be very, very happy and I would have a sense of humor, a little bit ironic. It would be funny. It would be very funny because it would be like a little joke I have with myself. It would be very playful. In reality, if I did not need anything, if I did not assume that I need something from the outer world, I think that for the first time in my life I would really be able to contribute to this world.

Pedro: Wow.

Violet: You know what I mean?

Pedro: Oh, I do.

Violet: And in this playfulness, in this big paradox there is joy and laughter and creativity. And the main thing, humor, laughter would arise. It would make this a wonderful, wonderful experience of being a human being.

Pedro: Yes.

Violet: Only in this case I can imagine human existence as a gift. Otherwise, it's torture. Yeah.

Pedro: So, what is now new, fresh, clear, even exciting, Violet, that was not there before this inquiry? What did you discover in this session?

Violet: That this pain of being separated is an illusion, that it does not exist, and that I am sometimes so desperate because I just imagine that I do not have the things that I need. It is clear to me now that I am searching for these things in places where they do not exist. I discovered that I do have a lot already and I should be more grateful for what I have in life, I really do have a lot and when I am confused, I'm not grateful for this. This is new. What is new is also this hellish image that I have of being alone. This is new. I realize that it is important to cultivate, to live my life in a way where daily I really look, I really care that I have experiences where I am connected with myself, for example, in nature, and that I nourish myself, that I fulfill my needs for myself, that I nurture my inner world. So really new and exciting is to not be afraid. To not focus on the outcome world. To make your inner world your priority and move towards this inner space and really seek for what you would do to nurture and cultivate this inner world. It would be important for me to become a good gardener of my inner land, and that I learn the skills; that I really learn the skills and be able to differentiate what has to be removed and what do I want to cultivate. What is my garden? What color is it? Which plants shall I grow to be a good gardener? Yeah. Ah, new, I get a gardener for my inner land. Yeah. Yeah. It's beautiful.

Pedro: So how is this issue actually an opportunity? How is this pain actually a door opener?

Violet: It is a very profound door opener because I have realized in this session that the fear is projected to the outer world, and it is a big disservice to us to look for something in the outer world when the cause of the lack is created in the inner world. You know what I mean? It's not completely exactly formulated, but it's a big confusion. It's really not realizing how life actually works. The mind projects its fears or its images. So the world is a projection of the mind, and I am looking for fulfillment within experiences that are made up with my mind. This is not possible. So I just have to be a good gardener and cultivate my inner garden and I can let go of the other things. I need not to worry about bosses and lovers and all these things. I really not need to.

Pedro: All the characters we make up, right? All the characters we make up that we are convinced we need in order to be nurtured in this world. And as we look for those, we miss the nurturing that we already have.

Violet: Yes, all the roles, you know. I do not have to be interested in this illusion. I can really let it go. Taking care of the illusion is not my job. I must care about my inner state of mind. This is the only thing that I have to do, and the other things, I can release. This is the only thing.

Pedro: So Violet, I need something from the outside. How valid is this issue after this inquiry from 0 to 10?

Violet: It's a 2.

Pedro: So what is in the gap between 2 and 0? What is left there still that is getting in the way of you having a direct and clear experience of zero?

Violet: I do not believe that I am whole. This is... I...

Pedro: Yes, and this "I" runs on the assumption that you are not whole. And because you innocently affirm inside that you are not whole, then how can you be at peace with yourself?

Violet: Yes.

Pedro: And when you assume that you are not whole, who do you turn into, Violet? Who do you become when you are validating that you are not whole?

Violet: I become someone who needs something from the outside. Again. Yeah.

Pedro: And who do others turn into in your mind?

Violet: They turn into givers or not givers, into those who fill the whole or do not. Into objects.

Pedro: So, let me invite you to close your eyes and take a deep breath and notice when you turn into the one that is not whole and others turn into the ones that get in the way of that wholeness, what do you miss? Just stay there. What are you not able to see when you are validating that you are not whole?

Violet: I miss that I am interconnected with everything, that I am part of a net.

Pedro: Where do you feel that interconnectedness in your body?

Violet: I feel it in the border of my body, in the outer space of the body. I feel it as form, as my outer form. So, I feel it... I am a form that seems to be paradoxically separated from others.

Pedro: And what do you miss when you are experiencing it as a form that is separated from others? Just stay there and notice.

Violet: What do I miss?

Pedro: Yes, what do you miss?

Violet: When I think I am separated from the others?

Pedro: Yes.

Violet: I miss the biological processes as though I'm part of nature. We all come from nowhere and go into nowhere, so I definitely miss the origin and the return as we are in the same cycle of life. And I am the product of other people. So, it's not possible that I exist for myself because I've been born, I've been born from a man and a woman, and I am alive. Yeah, so in essence, there are a lot of people around me. I'm clearly not able to survive alone. I'm a social being. I already experience others to survive, and everything is organized like this, regardless of wanting or getting something from them or not. So, I'm in a net, interwoven in a net of... Yeah.

Pedro: So how would you live now without validating that you are not whole?

Violet: Oh I would be very happy. My body would be very alive. Every cell of the body would sparkle. Also there comes a sense of humor. I would appreciate myself more, much more and I would see also uniqueness of others and myself much more. I would enjoy life and I would have deep trust in life because I'm whole and I'm not separated from life. This wholeness would not be destroyed, would not be destroyed, yes. No fear of life. No fear of death. A lot of happiness, a lot of connectedness, a lot of laughter and also thankfulness to be alive and considering life as a gift to make unique experiences in a space that is highly creative and full of forms. Life would be also very entertaining.

Pedro: So, Violet, let me invite you to close your eyes and take a deep breath and really allow yourself to recognize with every cell in your body, this space of trust, of wholeness, and joy that you are experiencing right now, and to recognize it with your whole body, your entire body, all the way to the deepest center of your being.

Breathe. Take a deep breath. And as you do that, allow yourself to relax into that space. Don't try to hold on to it. Don't try to recreate it. Don't try to save it in a little bag. Just relax into it. Relax into this trust, relax into this wholeness, relax into this joy, and breathe. And as you recognize this space of trust, love, and joy, simply radiate it; expand it. Notice how your body naturally expands this recognition and this relaxation. And breathe and rest in this experience.

So, Violet, in this experience, how valid is it that you are not whole on a scale of 0 being nothing and 10 being max?

Violet: It's zero.

Pedro: So, I invite you to recognize this zero, relax into this zero, and expand this zero [Long pause]. How would you describe the experience of Zero, Violet?

Violet: It's the formless dimension within myself. I experienced it as expansion, as highly vibrant and at the same time full of stillness. It is very still and at the same time it is fully dynamic and it's extremely peaceful and it's an expansion of the mind and I can also perceive it as light.

Pedro: So, from this space, Violet, what would you see as the naturally emergent next steps for you, if at all?

Violet: Regularly visit this space. Really, return to this dimension daily and yeah, to go on doing what I do. To really explore this space by studying, by contemplating, and by living my life, my everyday life in a joyful way, becoming a gardener of my inner landscape.

Pedro: Thank you, Violet. It was such a beautiful experience to join you in this process.

Violet: Thank you for leading me through this process.

Pedro: It's my joy.

Violet: Thank you, Pedro.

2

I Need to Know Where He Is

Tania: What would you like to look into today, Claude?

Claude: I think what I notice is that at very random times during the day, it could be any time of the day or night, I have a thought about my son, who is in college for the first time. He is in New York City. And I immediately experience a sensation of discomfort, anxiety in my body and the thought comes up, **I need to know where he is**. I have a queasy, uneasy feeling, and then I need to know where he is.

Tania: Where in your body do you experience this queasy feeling?

Claude: I'm experiencing it right now in my upper stomach area, It's in my guts. It's like a cold. My hands get cold and clammy, and I feel lightheaded. I feel kind of like a floating sensation all throughout my body, some tightness in my jaw, some clenching. It feels kind of like a sack that's enveloping my entire body, that's vibrating with some very slow … like thick liquid, like cold. It's kind of moving through my body, but also enveloping the space around my body. It's undulating. It's cold. It's pressing down somehow. It's gray and it has kind of a... It feels like at the center it has kind of a pull. It's pulling at me. It seems to coalesce right into my stomach.

Tania: And on a scale of 1 to 10, how valid is this issue for you?

Claude: It's an 8 or a 9.

Tania: And how do you validate this sensation in your body, and that you need to know where he is?

Claude: It seems to be alerting me to some danger. It seems to want to validate that there is danger. I have to get to him. Not even that I must get to him, it's more that I need to know where he is. That seems to be the thought that goes with the sensation and it's completely oblivious to my surroundings or anything that's actually going on. I could be talking to somebody, I could be driving in the car, I could be relaxing.

Tania: Who do you turn into in your mind when you are validating this bodily sensation, and you are validating that you need to know where he is? Who do you turn into in your mind?

Claude: I turn into the protector. I turn into a kind of like a security guard. Like I'm the cop, kind of like a policeman and a security guard and the responsible one. I'm responsible for his safety even if he is living in the city far away. I'm responsible for detecting any danger, any problems.

Tania: So when you turn into the protector, into the security guard, into the police man, who do others turn into? Who does he turn into?

Claude: He turns into a very vulnerable, absent-minded person. This is how he shows up in my mind. He is not aware of his surroundings. He is a bit helpless. But I see him in my mind with his phone hanging out of his pocket and his… like, his backpack open and he is walking around New York. So I turn him into somebody that is completely clueless, unaware of his surroundings and in needing protection. I feel like I could throw up.

Tania: So, when you experience yourself in this throwing-up space, when you are validating that sensation, how do you exaggerate, or disconnect or freeze?

Claude: That's nausea. That's not just nausea. I'm going to throw up! That is exaggeration. My mind is wanting to accentuate it, like, "Yeah. If you throw up, then it's really valid, it's really true, this feeling". How do I freeze with this bodily sensation? I notice a thought like "I can't go on like this. I've got to do something." This is an exaggeration. Then my mind starts battling: "Well, you can't call him because you agreed not to call until Sunday. You can't text him because then you are not giving him space. You can't check up on his phone, like, where is he? Because you don't want to like..." It's like I start going into these arguing modes. Should I? Shouldn't I? Should I? Shouldn't I? And all of it is validated by this physical sensation saying, "Do something!" So that feels overactive. And I freeze a little when I start thinking that I should call him or when should I call him? I just get in this maze inside my head about it. Another thing I'm noticing is that I freeze with this bodily sensation. I don't want to get up and move around. It kind of feels like I have to hunker down and just deal with it.

Tania: When you are validating this sensation in the body, the nausea, what is repetitive? What patterns can you see? What are the cycles that show up for you internally?

Claude: It feels like fear, fear and irrational responsibility. This repetitive "it's up to me", you know, there is a belief like his life is up to me. I'm the security guard. I'm responsible for keeping bad things from happening. That would be the repetitive cycle. And I'm left with this breakdown in my body. And that's repetitive. This idea is very childlike... I'm responsible for my sister's safety, I'm responsible for my parents' safety... You know, I was that kid, very vigilant. The Catcher in the Rye. Still in my work now as a therapist and a psychiatrist I feel that responsibility and that helplessness.

Tania: So, Claude, what assumptions are you making about this issue for yourself?

Claude: Oh! So many! I'm laughing! It's like swatting at a fly or something because the fly just zips by and it's this little thing. I'm like swatting my son! And I notice there are other feelings when I think of him. I miss him. I feel sad. I feel so happy for him. There are so many other emotions. But I keep swatting at this particular fly in front of my face imagining that he is in danger and it's my job to save him. That I'm responsible. This queasy body thing. I am creating that for sure.

Tania: And what assumptions are you making of others? How are you solidifying others?

Claude: Yeah. Well, I do. I notice that I feel a little anxious when I call him and my voice kind of goes up and I start asking him like, "Oh, what did you do?" and start acting on those fears. But I'm also like trying to rein it in a lot. It feels a little sped up and not really authentic and I'm not really listening. He sounds a little distant and I think, "Oh my gosh, is he in trouble? Is there a problem?" So, in that way, I don't know how he experiences it, but I know I experience it like a tense conversation.

Tania: So, let me invite you to close your eyes, Claude. Take a deep breath and ponder the following question without trying to answer it. Just ponder the question and wait for insight to come naturally, for clarity to be shown. What do you miss? What are you not able to see, to notice, when you are validating this sensation in your body, this nausea, this tension, this resistance in your body, when you are validating it, what are you missing?

Claude: [Prolonged silence.] What's coming up is this enormous freedom to not have to know where he is or when he is coming home or who he is with or what he is doing. That there is a lot of freedom, freedom and joy and space to just... just to be at peace in my body. I miss just how incredibly amazing it is that he is doing this. We are evolving our lives. It's fully embracing the change and just how miraculous it really is to have had this baby and 18 years later he is walking around New York City somehow feeding himself, getting on the subway, going to his classes, buying his breakfast, making friends, doing his laundry. So far, he seems to be doing pretty amazing. And I noticed I am too. I love coming home and having the space. I have a lot more time and I can just wander. It's incredible. So, I'm really not able to notice this when I'm validating these images and sensations in my mind, the queasy, security guard stuff. He does not belong to me. He is profoundly himself. He is profoundly free. He is free. I'm free and yet we are connected. We are so deeply and beautifully connected.

Tania: So, as you see this, how would you live your life without validating the sensation, the nausea, the resistance, and that tension? How do you live your life without validating all of that?

Claude: Oh gosh! Just more of what I've been in touch with when I'm in touch with it, which is just deeply following my interest, following... It's not even quite that. It's just fully being with whatever is in front of me, with whatever is happening here. That's how I would live. It's not doing something else. It's literally connecting with this space. I can feel so much tenderness about him and about our life and our family. I can really feel so much gratitude and the unfolding of all of our lives. That's very hard to put into words, but it's just that continuing, shifting, moving perpetually into this joining with everything that is here.

Tania: So, what is now new? What is exciting? What is fresh? What is clear that was not there before this inquiry?

Claude: Well, I just got my breath and my body back. What's new, what's fresh is my breathing is much deeper right now. My hands aren't cold. My whole-body temperature feels more just like regulated. What is new? This insight that, this reaction, this vigilance, this thing that seems to come up very quickly is also, I think is short-circuiting other emotions like being genuinely open to missing him. There is a sweet way of thinking about somebody that you love. Where are they? What are they doing? There is a sweetness that I'm really not getting in touch with when I'm on this security guard duty. I can find joy that he is in university classes, he is meeting friends and there is something very pleasant about that. And then it's also an insight for me to be just really in touch with excitement and joy of the things that are available to me now that I have more space for, literally. You know, working on all my plants in my office. I'm doing a lot of that these days. So yeah, that... I can see how I cheat myself out of that sweetness. Yeah.

Tania: So how, Claude, how is this nausea, how is this a tension, how is this being the security guard, this being the protector, how is all this actually an opportunity?

Claude: I just had this image of stepping out of the security guard role, like the hat and the coat and the uniform. It's an opportunity to get even closer to myself in those moments that I feel the nausea, that I feel the shortness of breath to really acknowledge the awe and the joy and the relief of having him out on his own relatively. It's an opportunity to really notice where I'm validating holding myself back from things that I want to do because I'm still his mom. You know, I still have the kid in college. You've got to be on top of all these things. And I noticed that I could use that to validate not taking certain risks in my life, particularly my work life. So, it's definitely an opportunity to dig into that, like what's holding me back?

Tania: Yes. Do you see any self-evident next steps, any movement that is naturally arising towards something? No effort here, just what do you see yourself naturally doing with this insight?

Claude: I notice the invitation to breathe more deeply. Actually, I notice some things like the action of just lying down or the action of getting really quiet. That's an action. The intention to get quieter and to remind myself that's really okay. It's really, really okay to give up this post, you know? I think it would look like in my encounters with him, to be really quiet with him, to listen more, not have an agenda in the conversation. Like there is this other thing of, well, we made this arrangement; we are only going to really talk on the phone once a week. So like, ah, ah, I got to get all this in. That would be pretty radical to show up in those conversations without the queasy feeling and without the, and just listening, connecting.

Tania: How valid is the original bodily sensation on a scale, zero being nothing and 10 being max.

Claude: The body sensation is a clear zero. I feel like I've been holding onto something and it now fully released.

Tania: So, let's help that process. Let me invite you to close your eyes for a second and take a deep breath and just really allow yourself to go deep into this Zerospace, to fully experience in every cell of your body. Just breathe and receive, allow and receive, recognize and relax into this space. Once you are there, allow yourself to expand it all the way to the core of your being and outside in all directions. When you are firmly there, let me know in your words how would you describe this?

Claude: It feels like being fully held. Moving in this very, very spacious, weightless, completely benign, like a... It's like a body of water. It just feels... It feels completely supported. There is just a very gentle, gentle drifting.

Tania: Thank you, Claude.

3

My Partner

Saylan: I would like to work on my relationship with my partner.

Pedro: Very well. So, tell me about that issue or that situation.

Saylan: Yeah, I would say, oh gosh, it's just so hard and so complex. My issue is it almost seems like he is two different people. He is just such a bright, amazing being. And then there is this side... He seems like two different people. And I reached this point where I tolerate and I actually have all these ways of making that behavior okay until it's just so not, and I'm making plans in my mind of how I can get out of it. The thought is I want out, I need out, I need to find a way. And then yeah, within that it's just feeling really trapped because we actually have such a beautiful life together. You know, it's our kids. But there is this side that is so toxic and this way of relating that I just can't basically manage anymore.

Pedro: Where do you experience this sensation in your body? Of being trapped?

Saylan: Yeah, I would say my solar plexus. I could really feel my solar plexus tightened as I was talking. I can actually feel a little bit of a gripping up into my heart area as well, in the back of my heart.

Pedro: If it had a color or a texture or a size, how would you describe it?

Saylan: Well, it's interesting. It almost looks like about the size of a hand or maybe two hands. Like one hand is really around my solar plexus and the other hand is more around the back of my heart, like that. It's like this brown, burgundy color.

Pedro: When you are validating this sensation in your body, of feeling trapped, what shows up in your mind?

Saylan: That I need to find a way out. Yeah, it's just, that's what I'm occupied with, it's really thoughts of how to get out.

Pedro: Who do you turn into, Saylan, in your mind, when you are validating that sensation in your body, of feeling trapped?

Saylan: I turn into someone who is really distracted,

limited. Yes, I can see how limited my perspective becomes in terms of focusing my energy on what I think needs to happen.

Pedro: If you think of a character or a role, who do you turn into when you are validating the sensation of feeling trapped?

Saylan: A character? I would say the victim. Yes, but it's like a victim determined not to be a victim. So, someone pushing their way to be free.

Pedro: When you turn into this victim that is determined to find freedom, who does he turn into? When you become this character or you embody this role, who does he turn into?

Saylan: He turns into someone to stay away from, avoid, a toxic energy that I don't want to be around. He turns into a threat.

Pedro: And so, when you are the brave victim that wants freedom, and he is the toxic one, and you are living in this role, and you are assigning him that role, how do you exaggerate, or disconnect, or freeze?

Saylan: I exaggerate by taking any little evidence that proves that he is toxic, any comment he makes and really hyper focus on it and play it again and again making it really big. And all of these negative criticism or comments just take up all the space. I can see how my system gets sped up, like almost into fight or flight when I'm around him and need to busy myself or need to do something. I get really worked up about it. Like desperate, like there is almost a desperation.

Pedro: Do you disconnect or freeze?

Saylan: I have more of the fight-flight kind of thing going on. But yes, I certainly disconnect from him. I often disconnect from my feelings and myself. I'll often actually busy myself with something that is totally disconnecting.

It's like I can't handle it, and there is nowhere to go. So I might as well just do nothing. But it will be like I'll be crocheting or something, even though I've got so many things to do. It's just too much to handle when I'm projecting those roles. Like life is too much to handle. So I see how I do actually disconnect and freeze.

Pedro: When you are validating those roles and you are validating this sensation in your body, feeling trapped, what is repetitive or what patterns show up for you internally?

Saylan: I often withdraw, and I start making my own plans of how I can take care of myself, how I can empathize with myself, how I can do it all on my own and just start making plans of caring for myself. I get further and further into it and more withdrawn, disconnected from him for sure.

But I don't actually take care of myself. I think of all these things I should be doing to take care of myself. There are thought patterns around how he is never going to support me to do these things that I need to do to take care of myself. So, I need to figure out a plan in terms of how to do that, but I don't actually do things in that moment to take care of myself.

Pedro: Yeah. So, what untested assumptions are you making around this issue?

Saylan: I'm assuming he doesn't love me or care about me. Actually, I'm assuming he despises me.

You know, little comments, because I generally don't talk to many people about it, but I do make these little comments about how he is going away for three months for example, and how it's easier with him gone. Thank goodness he is going for three months. I don't have to clean up after him. Or yeah, I'm not going to have to deal with his comments. I notice myself making little comments like that, that are letting others know how hard it is for me.

Pedro: Yes, it's interesting how it's not enough for us to validate a perception or an assumption, we also really like it when others validate that same assumption, and we do our best to convince them of it.

So, let me invite you to close your eyes, Saylan, and take a deep breath and ponder the following question without trying to answer it. Just ponder the question and wait for insight to come naturally. What do you miss? What are you not able to see when you are validating this sensation in your body, that you are feeling trapped? What do you miss when you are validating your role as an active victim, his role as someone toxic, and when you validate this experience of being desperate? When you are living this way, and you are filtering life through this lens, what do you miss? What are you not able to see? And just wait, and breathe, and notice.

Saylan: [Prolonged silence] I'm not able to see that this feeling of desperation actually originates inside me. I'm also not able to see the health of my support system. All this health that's surrounding it and actually the health that's within it. And there is a sense of clarity around the wisdom of my system.

I miss what that this health in my support system is actually connected with the earth. I recognize I'm not alone and I'm not an isolated being. I miss the vastness of that connection. So I miss this sense of freedom that I am so intimately connected with and equally, if not more, a part of me, or who I actually am.

Pedro: So Saylan, how would you live now, how would you engage with yourself and others without validating this sensation in your body of feeling trapped?

Saylan: I would live through a wider lens. One where I'm seeing everybody and everything from all angles. I would live my life through this greater sense of connection and in that connection, I would feel gratitude for everyone in my life and the roles they play. I can really notice the softness.

There is a softer, wider view.

Pedro: How would you relate to him without validating this sensation in your body, that you are feeling trapped?

Saylan: With more of an open-eye curiosity. I recognize how I avoid him with my eyes and with my presence. So I would relate to him by actually looking at him and receiving him with more open curiosity and without running away from my experience of him at the same time. Yes.

Pedro: Now visualize him in front of you. What can you now see about him, about you, about your relationship when you do not validate this sensation in your body that you are trapped? In your mind, look at him in the eyes, take a deep breath, and ask yourself what is now clear for you without validating that sensation in your body?

Saylan: Just a really clear sense of where all the drama comes from. What is clearer is how much more is there surrounding, holding, witnessing within and around the pattern or the holding, the tightness, the contraction. Yes, I'm just able to see with more clarity all of the resources I have available and the beauty around me. Yes.

Pedro: So how is this sensation of feeling trapped in your body actually an opportunity?

Saylan: It's an opportunity to connect with myself and to connect with a deeper, wider space and perspective. It's an opportunity to step back beyond the movie and the drama and hold a bigger picture. It's just an opportunity to actually find movement and healing and new life and potential.

Pedro: What specific and concrete next steps are now clear for you? And by clear I mean transparently self-evident, without any effort

Saylan: Yes. It feels like a deep nurturing of this wider sense of universal support, like sitting in this place of witnessing and holding that specific understanding. This feels really like cultivating, practicing, being in that space of clarity, whether I'm in his presence or not, but especially bringing that into my interaction with him.

Pedro: Yeah. So on a scale of 0 being nothing and 10 being max, how valid is this sensation in your body still after this inquiry?

Saylan: It's about a 3.

Pedro: Where would you say you started, Saylan?

Saylan: Probably like a 9.

Pedro: Okay. So what's still behind the 3?

Saylan: There is a sense of it being manageable now, yet it's still a burden.

Pedro: A burden. Ok. And who do you turn into when you validate that it's still a burden?

Saylan: I turn into the responsible one; the one that needs to take care of everything. I'm the one that has to do the work. And yeah... it's the pattern. It's how it is. I'm the one who has to clean up the messes, deal with the kids, keep the wider perspective so everything goes okay. Yes, I got this. It's manageable. I can do it. And then it's just like, fuck this. Why do I have to take care of everything? Why is it always me that has to do all the work?

Pedro: And what do you miss Saylan, when you are validating that it's still a burden? Ponder this question and wait. What do you miss when you are validating that it's still a burden?

Saylan: I miss, somehow, it's like I miss *seeing*... It's so funny, I miss having some enjoyment. I miss the enjoyment of the circumstance. I don't know if that makes sense. I miss enjoying what's there to be lived in the experience itself without wanting a particular outcome.

Pedro: What do you miss about him? What are you not able to see about him when you are validating that it's still a burden?

Saylan: I'm not able to see the perfection of what he is showing me, the experience that he is offering me to experience. Yes, I'm not able to be grateful for the clarity I am getting about him and what is not working for me about him when I'm validating that it's still a burden.

Pedro: So how is this burden actually an opportunity for you?

Saylan: It's an opportunity for me to actually have something to push against or relate with, to play with, to be creative around, to grow. Exactly, to leverage, to use, to grow, to understand, yes.

Pedro: What a beautiful plan, like a perfect curriculum for each of us. So how is it that your partner is your perfect curriculum right now?

Saylan: He just really provides that friction and resistance that I need to grow. I need that to know who I am, to know who he is, and to know what is possible and not possible about our relationship. It's like I'm here to meet, to be solid, and to play with matter and to discover who we really are beyond our projections. And that includes resistance and friction and bumping up against different parts. There is this sense of more play, discovery, adventure, joy and laughter

Pedro: What is new after everything you have discovered in this inquiry? What resources do you actually have?

Saylan: It's just interesting because I can feel all that clarity and power. Confusion feels distant. I don't feel like I'm in it anymore. I'm just like, wow, I'm integrating everything. So, there is now space and breath.

Pedro: Saylan, let me invite you to recognize this

spaciousness, to relax into the spaciousness and to expand the spaciousness internally all the way into the last cell of your body, to your bone marrow, and outwardly in all directions.

[Prolonged silence]

So "It's still a burden." How valid is this issue on the scale of 0 to 10.

Saylan: Yes, zero. I'm not feeling the burden of it at all.

4

I Lost Myself

Daniel: Let's talk about sex. About when my partner tells me she has pain and doesn't want sex and to please respect that. And I feel trapped because I don't want to have another woman. I don't want to go to other people.

I'm very respectful and I feel a lot. I am a perfectionist into really creating a space where she can feel safe. I did it for a decade, 10 years. And I'm fed up with it. I think it will never come to an end. And this creates even more pain. I think **I have lost myself** doing this. You know, I'm always trying to improve this caretaker role to my own self detriment.

Tania: And how do you validate that you have lost yourself?

Daniel: Because I am stuck now, I don't know what to do. I don't. I feel helpless and I don't have any clue how to react and how to act. I am afraid of doing something and I am afraid of not doing something, both at the same time. It is horrible. When I have in mind that we should have sex, then I think that we shouldn't. And when there is more chance, I won't, and then there is no chance. So, I just learned that I won't go there, period. So, I lost contact with myself and with her. And now I am petrified of going into that space and I don't even know if I want to or don't want to go into that space. I feel stuck, afraid, and resentful.

Tania: So, who do you turn into in your mind, Daniel, when you are validating this experience around sex?

Daniel: Generally, a victim, and when I would like to have sex then like if I was some kind of abuser. Someone that would hurt her inherently just by wanting to have sex. So, in essence, I reduce myself to someone inadequate and then I'm a victim again.

Tania: And who does she turn into in your mind when you are that victim?

Daniel: She also turns into some kind of abuser. She abuses her power, her victimhood, her control. She has that power in her hand to do whatever she wants with me internally. She has the power, and she is just waiting patiently to use it. For me, it's a 10 out of 10. You know, it's really a 10. On a scale of 1 to 10, it's really a... it's really a 12! It could be also a 20. Yes!

Tania: So when you are validating these issues around sex, and they are a 20 in a scale of 1 to 10, how do you exaggerate, disconnect or freeze?

Daniel: I exaggerate by always flipping between being sensitive and careful and then wanting sex, and then hating myself for it. So, in essence I exaggerate between wanting to kind of kill myself or to completely forget about myself. There are only two worlds in this mindset, and they are both horrible.

Tania: What is repetitive? What's cyclical? You started mentioning a little bit about certain patterns. When you are validating this issue around sex, what is repetitive, what is cyclical, what patterns do you see, Daniel?

Daniel: The biggest pattern I see is either being the caretaker or losing and hating myself. There is absolutely no room for anything else. The pattern is really losing myself. Not knowing who or what I am.

Tania: And what untested assumptions are you making around this issue?

Daniel: Well assuming I should be loved! By having the desire to receive love! Especially in a situation where that, receiving love, is not happening. This is how I create it as an issue for myself. I create it by going into the past, knowing that I had it in the past and wanting it back. And waiting. Thinking okay, I just need to wait for a few hours, or a few days, or a few years, or a few decades. If I wait it will come back. I create it because I think it could happen again.

Tania: So, let me invite you to close your eyes Daniel, and take a deep breath and ponder the following question without trying to answer it. Just ponder the question and wait for insight. What do you miss? What are you not able to see when you are validating this issue?

Daniel: I am not able to see me. And I am not able to see the extreme, devastating tiredness I feel. And the heaviness. I can't feel the heaviness. I'm not able to stay alone and to be peaceful with myself alone. I'm not able to really dive deep and connect with myself and with the world inside. I'm not able to connect with her. And also, you know, to connect with this tenderness, to live this tenderness and this openness, this being open. I miss openness. Openness towards life, towards mystery in life, towards what's happening now. And I miss home, rooted in myself or in my source. I missed the source of my life.

In the end, I miss life itself and by doing that I miss my own sexuality. I miss this feeling of me being whole, in peace. I miss the experience of being one with everything here. I miss this abundance of life. And I miss receiving her intimacy even with a "No" coming from her. I miss her beauty even in her unwillingness to have sex. It's like I miss life itself.

I miss the joy of living life, not knowing what's happening next. I miss living life with the curiosity and the openness of not deeply knowing life itself and not having any power over it. In the end I miss Love. Love with a capital "L". Yes, I see. I miss this inherent love arising from existence itself without the need to create it, and without the need to feed it, or administer it, or manipulate it. Without the need to overpower it and of wanting to do something with it instead of just feeling powerless and completely in love with life as it is. I miss the love of life that is already there without me needing to do anything about it, and I miss myself.

Tania: So how would you live now? Considering everything you've seen so far, how would you live your life with all this knowing?

Daniel: With all this clarity. It finally feels that I can breathe. It feels like I'm just receiving an internal miracle from myself just now. It feels like an opening and radiant heart. I feel like a huge oxygen flow coming into my lungs and oxygen-rich blood pumping through my veins. It feels like a vast, deep, peaceful and supportive inner space is growing, and widening, and expanding. A deep understanding of how I exist. It's like really coming home. I connect with myself and feel... I feel at home.

Tania: And what is now fresh, new, clear, or even exciting that was not there before this inquiry?

Daniel: Now, when I see her in my mind, I see her in her beauty. In her beauty and tenderness. Exactly as she is, and I want her to be exactly that. Exactly who she is. It's like I see her for the very first time without my filters and projections, and I see her as such a tender soul, and she is so beautiful being who she believes to be. It feels like I can just sit next to her with myself, with my openness, taking responsibility of my desire, and of my power, and just sit watching her without wanting anything from her. Without a single expectation, or assumption. It's just full intimacy now happening. This is a space where I am connected to myself, to her, to the world, to everyone, to life, to joy, to transcendence, to some kind of deeper knowing and deeper understanding. I'm whole! I'm complete!

This experience is not one where she either needs to win or I need to win. It's like a third thing that's happening between us, and I just follow it. And it could also be in silence. And I just notice how beautiful she is, how beautiful we are. And I stay in this, my inner world of seeing the beauty, and it feels like a more expansive form of love comes back. It's an intimacy of connecting and being curious about what is next without any expectations, without any plan, without any script. Opening up to what's next, and next, and then go from there.

Tania: So how is this issue actually an opportunity for you?

Daniel: It is an opportunity to receive this form of eternity and to practice how to step into this eternity, into this flow of consciousness letting all other distractions, assumptions, projections, disappointments go.

Tania: So, let me invite you to close your eyes and internally open up to this experience and to fully receive it in your body. And as you fully receive it Daniel, tell me how valid is this issue of losing yourself on a scale of 0 being nothing and 10 being max?

Daniel: It is still a one.

Tania: And what can you find behind this one?

Daniel: It is that I need a physical experience.

Tania: And how do you validate that you need a physical experience?

Daniel: It's a longing for another physical body and also for touch. There is still a lack of this.

Tania: And who do you turn into in your mind when you validate that you need an experience with a physical body, and you are not having it? Who do you turn it into?

Daniel: Oh, heavy. Oh, heavy. It is so heavy. It's so hard. It becomes devastating, the waiting, and it feels closed down forever.

Tania: And who do other people turn into in your mind when you are validating that you need a physical experience and you are not having one?

Daniel: I turn into a really needy person, and they turn into people who could potentially fulfill this need.

Tania: And when you are in this mind space, what is repetitive, cyclical, or pattern like?

Daniel: This wanting, this thinking that this wanting is love and that I'm not enough, that I'm not enough to have it. This thinking that I need somebody as a body, in the literal sense of it. I need my body and I need another body to be complete. And the pattern is, the pattern is really shutting myself down and feeling this heaviness of not receiving it fully.

Tania: So, let me invite you to take a deep breath, Daniel. Take a deep breath and ponder the following question: When you are validating that you need the physical experience of another body, what are you missing? What are you not able to notice?

Daniel: I miss the reality of what is actually being delivered by the Universe. I miss the reality that bodies and minds do not work like that. That no amount of wanting, projecting or hoping for anything is going to make it happen just because it is wanted. I miss peace, contentment, joy, understanding. I miss understanding. Yes, and also when I'm actually having sex, I also miss the actual event that is actually happening then because I am trapped in my own mind projecting all kinds of drama and scenarios. And in the end, I again miss Love. I totally miss the joyful, complete, uninterpreted moment.

Tania: So how would you live now without validating that you need a physical experience that you are not having?

Daniel: I would feel transparent. I would feel what's alive now and allow it to go through me. In this space there is no shame anymore. The shame is lifting. And I can stay raw, and vulnerable, and tender, and being hurt, and touched, or not touched. And the tears. I feel just overwhelmed by this sensation of openness.

How would I live now? Kindly, and spontaneously, and honestly, and lovingly, and without a hidden agenda, just saying whatever needs saying with all the kindness in the world and then leaving it there in the hands of the universe for whatever needs to happen or not to happen without any interference from me.

Tania: So how valid is this issue from 0 to 10, I need a physical experience?

Daniel: Yes, not so valid anymore.

Tania: So, what's still left? It could also be a sensation in the body?

Daniel: Well, before it was "I need a physical sensation from her body" and now it is "I need a physical sensation from my body", yes.

Tania: You need a physical sensation from your body. So, what do you miss, what are you not able to see, when you are validating that you need this physical sensation from your own body?

Daniel: I miss my actual body! This one I actually do have right here, right now! Oh, I miss this very tender and amazing, and powerful sense of existence! It's like I miss receiving this deeper understanding of the universe, this intuition or original soul or… there are no words for this actually. It's just deep reconnection, being unquestionably plugged in.

Tania: So how would you live now Daniel without validating that you need a body?

Daniel: I would live plugged in. Infinite. Knowing. Clear. Peaceful. Whole. Joyful. Complete. Unquestionably plugged in.

Tania: How does that feel in your body right now?

Daniel: It's very difficult to talk about this. It feels like an infinite, unnamable, expansive, and also very concrete and grounding space at the same time ... It's like light. It is more tender than light actually. I feel completely held. It feels ecstatic.

Tania: So how valid is it that you need a body on a scale of 0 to 10.

Daniel: Zero.

Tania: If there were any words to describe this Zerospace, how would you describe it?

Daniel: It's light and laughter. It's peace and clear action both at the same time. It's knowing life beyond appearances, assumptions, and projections. It is completeness. It's just so light and easy. There is no heaviness anymore in this body. It's like I get to have my body and at the same time I get to be free of it! Before it was more like child play, but now it feels more like embodying this depth of knowing and leaving this distracting playing zone, being a true grown up and taking real responsibility for whatever shows up internally, using this transformational power to help heal the world.

5

He Never Cared About Me

Eade: He never really cared about me.

Pedro: What else shows up for you when you are validating that he never cared about you?

Eade: I'm a fool. I was so stupid. I should have known better. I should have seen what was happening. I should have protected my daughter. I didn't matter. I was codependent. He is a narcissist. He only cared about himself. My heart is so tight. It's like someone has just gone in and carved it out. It's so tight and it's hard to breathe. My whole chest is really tight. It's not really my stomach, which is rare, but my whole chest is really tight, and my throat is very tight. It hurts. It feels like it's very choked up. I just feel… It's funny, like I'm sitting, but I kind of feel like I don't even have a lower half of my body. Like my legs aren't… They don't even feel real. It's not a sensation I've noticed before and I feel like my back is just really exposed. Yeah, there is no solidity under me or behind me. Free floating, but not in a good way, ungrounded.

Pedro: If this sensation in your body had a color, a texture, a size, what would it be?

Eade: It's several different shades of green. They are kind of blended. They are jagged on the ends, sharp on the ends and it's like the color doesn't fill the space. It's a little bit kind of frozen-ish or glass-like, still, and smooth and kind of glass-like, but it has a frozen texture to it.

Pedro: When you are validating this sensation in your body, who do you turn into in your mind?

Eade: Oh, a total victim. Yes, just a back fully exposed, someone who has no support, no foundation, no grounding, no solidity, someone who is weak and vulnerable and fragile. Yeah, really vulnerable. It's like I should just give up, just surrender.

Pedro: And when you turn into that, who do others turn into?

Eade: He is the one with all the power. He is solid. He is standing over me. He is very solid. It's funny. It's like I don't really matter to him other than he becomes someone who just wants to make sure I am kept down. He is just doing it with a little hand gesture and he is ruling his kingdom over here and I'm very small in the big scheme of things just so long as I'm kept down. So, he becomes my oppressor.

Pedro: When he becomes the oppressor and you become

the victim and you are validating this sensation in your body, how do you overreact? How do you exaggerate? How do you disconnect? How do you freeze?

Eade: I am just frozen. There is a paralysis, like I can't really move. It's funny this feeling I haven't noticed before of not having legs. That's what that is. I can't just walk myself out of here. I overreact by believing that we will always be in this position. He will always have the power. I'll always be the victim. I will never know how to get my power back from him. I overreact by playing it out for the next 40 years and him thriving, and me dwindling away. I see him and my daughter having some beautiful flourishing relationship, and she doesn't want to be with me. I'm just pathetic.

I disconnect from my power, or my strength, or my inner knowing, or my trust in life. I'm so disconnected from me. I have no power to give myself a reality check. It's just powerlessness. I'm so disconnected from me, it's like the powerlessness comes after the disconnecting. I disconnect because I don't want to be connected to this pathetic victim with no legs. I don't want anything to do with her.

I overreact by staying focused on him in the past, and what has been, and reinforcing or validating or saying that I'm learning about narcissism now when actually, I'm really just compulsively focused on narcissism, believing I have to learn every last thing of it in order to ever stand up to him. I have to completely overcome codependency in general, I have to spot every narcissist everywhere and put them out of my life, cut ties with every narcissist. I'm in that place of, you know, you are going to buy a certain car and then you see that car everywhere and now everywhere I look, there are narcissists.

I'm overreacting or exaggerating by saying he never cared about me. I'm convinced he is a narcissist. So that means he just only cares about himself. So I'm exaggerating and making that mean that he didn't care about me ever at all. Actually, I have no idea, but it seems I'm sure about it somehow. And it's not enough that he cared as much as he could. I'm exaggerating or overreacting to say that wasn't enough.

Pedro: So, when you are validating him as an oppressor, you as a victim, when you are validating this sensation in your body and thoughts like, he never cared about me, what's repetitive? What's cyclical? What patterns come up for you?

Eade: There were times in our marriage where I called him my oppressor. Being a victim is so familiar to me in this lifetime with my dad, wanting my dad to show up a certain way, wanting my ex to show up a certain way, thinking that if I just do this more or do this less, they will be able to show up and love me in the way I want to be loved. It's repetitive and cyclical just to be focused on him, focused on the dynamics around me, trying to understand it. I'm even still trying to fix it in the past now. Even if before it was trying to undo different things, now that I know this, I want to undo this pattern in the past. I want to go back and not be that person.

I want to come up with a strategy to protect myself from him in the future. Bulletproof myself to his tactics, putting the focus and the attention on him and it's pattern-like, not putting my attention on what I can actually change. However much I'm using that to just simply distract from pain, or guilt, or shame, or sadness, grief. That focusing on him means I don't have to focus on my own healing or my own part in it, and whatever emotions, pain and sadness, grief are up for me. Comparing myself, other women, men to him, relationships, our relationship to other relationships, always trying to figure out what is going on. It's so pattern-like, trying to figure this out so I can fix it and change it.

Pedro: When you are experiencing yourself as a victim and you are experiencing him as an oppressor and you are experiencing this sensation in your body and you are validating thoughts like he never cared about me, when you are doing all this, what untested assumptions are you making?

Eade: I am building and constantly repeating this to myself. I'm deciding what that means. He doesn't care about me. He never cared about me. He is not capable of caring. I picked the wrong person. I picked a bad person. There is something very wrong with me. Yes, that's what's the biggest thing in this. Whew, yeah, something is wrong with me! I picked the wrong person! I picked a bad person! I picked someone who is literally incapable of caring! Oh yeah, there is something wrong with me. I'm broken. Yeah, that's the bottom line. I'm creating it with that assumption.

I'm talking about it with everybody. I'm feeding it. Just running into someone in the store last night and she said, "Oh, I love the way you and your ex made your public announcement on Facebook about divorcing". I said, "Oh, it was all a scam and a fraud. None of it was true". And then I launched into the story. Everywhere I can find a way to bring it up, it's getting brought up.

Oh, and I love it when other people tell me, like the woman last night, "Oh, I could have told you that. A Narcissist for sure. I knew that. I mean, you didn't know that?" Most of the people I talked to said, "Oh, I could have told you that". I'm like, "Then why didn't you?"

Pedro: So let me invite you to close your eyes, Eade and take a deep breath and ponder the following question without trying to answer it. Just ponder the question and wait for clarity, for insight to show up on its own. When you are validating these roles, victim, oppressor, when you are validating this sensation in your body, when you are validating these thoughts, like, he never cared for me, what do you miss? What are you not able to see? What are you not able to notice? What becomes inaccessible to you when you are validating the sensation in your body, the roles and the thoughts?

Eade: I miss his innocence. I missed this wounded child who is blindly handling his childhood wounds. I'm missing that he literally doesn't know he is doing this. It's not to hurt me. I said it before a little bit, just that I'm missing that he has cared about me as much as he is capable of caring about someone, like literally as much as he is capable of. And that may definitely not be enough for me.

Pedro: How would that be clear to you?

Eade: He stayed for 22 years, and it wasn't an easy marriage. He always took care of us. He was always the primary breadwinner. He was always making sure we were okay as a family. He wanted to be a good dad. It was like he was dropped off from another planet and he didn't really know how to do certain things. So, I would tell him where to be, and when, and whatever with our daughter and he would always show up. He didn't know how to do things on his own in terms of showing up as a great dad, but if I said, be here on this day and do this, he did. He never missed anything our daughter did, ever.

He didn't know how to. He didn't know how to be in a family. Wow. But he wanted to. He wanted a family. He wanted to be there in our family. He wanted that. He just literally... Wow, he just literally did not know how to do it! Like, if you dropped me off at his office and said, you know, sell these products on Amazon, I mean, I don't know how to do that. He didn't either.

I see that he really wanted to be acknowledged for trying or for wanting to do it, even though he could rarely deliver on a lot of things. He wanted to be seen and acknowledged for trying. And I couldn't see and acknowledge that it wasn't enough, but dude, you've got to show up. He really did the best he could, and it just wasn't enough.

Pedro: So, what are you now able to see in regard to your entire relationship that you were not able to see before this inquiry?

Eade: That he had his ways of showing up. He didn't take care of me when I was sick or ever once bring me a glass of water in our whole married life, but he provided for us. That's what his dad taught him as a dad does. That's all he knew. Dads don't get their wives a glass of water or take care of them when they are sick, but they provide for them. And then what he was taught was dads defraud their wives and take everything in the divorce. But in the marriage, he provided. That was what he knew to do. That was his way of showing up. And he believed he was showing up completely.

He was raised by an alcoholic who was also a narcissist, and he was cautious around being codependent, and he thought getting someone a glass of water was being codependent. And he didn't want to do that. I can see that. I can see from here a struggle in him, a push and a pull of wanting to be a particular kind of person and literally not being able to be and wanting it. That was as much effort as could go into it and never being able to hit the mark. What a struggle. What a struggle that would be!

He knew that there was something off about him and he couldn't fix it. I just see such a wounded kid, a child whose parents just that created a lot of wounding, and it's just a defense mechanism, a way to survive. I see the innocence and I see mostly the kid, and I see a man who wants more and can't have it because he doesn't have the basics to access it. He wants things: love, connection, family, whatever it is and just simply can't have it. It's like I really see the want clearly, more clearly than I think I have ever, this longing for that.

I'm missing that. We were just perfect puzzle pieces. We both wanted certain things. We both made sacrifices and compromises. We both thought we would get the things we wanted from each other. Wow. I'm missing that we both got what we wanted! Wow. All of our goals, we manifested together. Yeah, I'm missing that he is an absolute master at all of the things that would keep me from being able to see what was happening, and I can also see my own innocence. I often say I'm stupid, and I should have seen this, and I should have known better. And I just absolutely couldn't see I,t and I didn't want to see it. Impossible.

I was totally willing to trade all of this for my family, turn a blind eye, ignore red flags. And I would do it all over again. I was not able to see what I was definitely not able to see. And what I'm missing is that we created so much good together and I wouldn't trade it. I am missing that I have a lot of love for him, and I'm not sure if that's stupid or not at this point, but it's there.

Yeah, I see that I can have whatever relationship with him I want moving forward so long as I have my freedom and my awareness, my eyes open. I don't have to avoid him for the rest of my life, which is what I thought I would have to do and the only way I could protect myself. He is just playing out a part for me. Oh gosh.

In some way I can see he is doing this for me. For my growth. It's some form of gift. Oh, I can really see this is so much bigger than him, so much bigger than me. I've been a prisoner to my own codependency this whole life. I haven't lived an authentic life because of me. I always see life as a chessboard and I'm a piece and you are a piece and he is a piece, and God just moves our pieces on the board and it's just perfect. I see I really did get everything I wanted. I don't want to perpetuate narcissism, but somehow I feel like bowing down to him in gratitude for the learning.

Pedro: And considering all you are noticing, and you are seeing right now, how would you live now?

Eade: I really would be grateful to him, specifically for where I am now, for what I have and for where I've gotten to. I'm grateful for him and for what we've created together, what we are continuing to destroy together. I would live my life much less as a victim, much more as an innocent person finding her way.

I see it in this moment as two steps forward and one step back, and two steps forward and one step back, but it's a dance and it's a two-step dance. And in a dance, there is actually no backwards. It's just that you have to go backward to make it a dance instead of just a walk. And so, the two forward and one back actually just makes it a dance. And I see the complete innocence of it. I would live my life freer to dance instead of thinking I have to just keep walking and moving forward. Thinking that there can never be a step back. Slowing down a little bit, being with what is now, not thinking that I'm not going to be okay until this is resolved one way or another.

Pedro: So, Eade, what's new? What's clear? What's fresh? What's even exciting that was not there before this inquiry?

Eade: I really see that I got every single thing I wanted. I see both of our innocence. I see the part he is playing. I see him as an actor with a role and a costume. Really seeing how much he wanted the things that I wanted him to want, but he couldn't make them happen. The wanting of it wasn't enough. I see that the wanting of it was so big and that was as close as he could get. He really did want to show up a certain way.

That image of two steps forward and one step back, that I don't have to just be on a mission to get somewhere is deeply liberating. Life is as a dance. So, we move here and then we are there, and it's so much more in the flow. There is no flow that's always moving forward. Wow. There is a flow and there is an ebb, and so it's like I could join the flow and the ebb. I feel more spaciousness to put my attention on me. Not to fix and heal and solve something, but to put my attention on me. Just how would I show up for me right now? What would I do for me? I'm just putting my attention on me. Less attention and focus on him and more on me.

Pedro: So how is this issue actually an opportunity?

Eade: I've been the victim to codependency. I've been affected, negatively impacted, limited by my codependency my whole life. I want to be done with that. If this is the opportunity to stop putting everybody else first, I don't know what better opportunity I could ever hope to have. Breast cancer for me was about weaning everybody off. If you don't do that because of breast cancer, you will have other opportunities apparently. Having experienced breast cancer, I didn't wean everybody off of me. So here I am getting this opportunity. And it's like so many leeches sucking off of me in so many ways that I'm just being inauthentic. It's like to just pull off of those, all of those off of me and stop nurturing everybody else and show up so much more authentically. Best opportunity ever!

Pedro: So Eade, from this space, do you see any clear, self-evident next steps for you? No trying, no wanting to do something, just things that show up as absolutely self-evident and natural to move into.

Eade: I think this is it, actually bowing down to him in freedom and independent gratitude and thanks for all that has been, and all that is, and all that is yet to come, and then just being done with that. Like not an everyday "I have to be grateful of that", but a one-time sincere, totally authentic bow. And when that bow is complete. Getting up, walking away, and moving forward. Turning away from that and focusing now on me.

Pedro: At this point, how valid is the original issue after this inquiry, zero being nothing and 10 max? How valid is the assignment of yourself as a victim, of him as an oppressor? How valid is this body sensation, and this notion that he never cared about you, from 0 to 10 right now?

Eade: It's a 2.

Pedro: And what is still behind that 2?

Eade: It shouldn't have taken me to lose everything to get this.

Pedro: It shouldn't have taken you to lose everything to get this. How do you validate this?

Eade: Well, I see images of the current lawsuit, the amount of money I've spent on it, the feeling of futility around it, seeing it drag out for years to come. No end in sight, images of my daughter not speaking to me this summer, being very angry with me and upset with me, believing her dad, taking his side. It shouldn't have taken losing everything. I mean, I see my financial situation, and I will run out of money with this lawsuit.

Pedro: And who would you turn into in your mind when you are validating this? Who do you transform into?

Eade: In this situation I'm angry, pissed off, a bitter ex-wife. Yeah, the bitter ex-wife who is in weird dynamics with the daughter and the ex, which I never imagined. The bitter ex-wife who is talking about him to other people, letting other people know what he has done, publicly talking about it. Who do I turn into? Yeah, the angry victim. The one who is hurtful or threatening him or badmouthing him or gathering proof against him, building a case against him.

Pedro: And when you are doing that, who does he turn into in your mind?

Eade: Well, I'm in a battle, so he becomes an opponent in a battle. He becomes someone I'm fighting and, in this case, he is a superior opponent. He has more money, better attorneys, strategy, a strategic mind. He is always figuring this out. He set it up. He intended to do all this. It's different than a worthy opponent. He is the one who is going to win regardless. I'm David actually, but I don't know if I'm going to win. I'm pretty scrappy, and he is pretty solid. He has got everything he needs to win.

Pedro: When you are validating these roles and assigning these roles to him and yourself, how do you exaggerate, disconnect, or freeze?

Eade: Just assuming this is a battle is an exaggeration. Yeah, I can see it in this moment, just seeing us in a battle makes it a battle instead of, well, we are letting the law figure out what's right. That's not actually a battle. Wow. I hadn't really seen that! I had really experienced being in a battle with him!

And I realize that I haven't lost everything. I still have my home. I have my daughter. I have myself and my life and my health and my inquiry and Zerospace. I haven't lost everything. I exaggerate by imagining that I will end up homeless because of attorney fees and so on. I exaggerate by believing this could go on forever. I don't even want to give myself any hope. I'm disconnected from hope or from trust or faith. All I've done is deal with this lawsuit for the most part. I'm freezing in terms of what it is that I want to be focusing on.

Pedro: So, what's repetitive? What's cyclical? What patterns can you see when you are validating that it shouldn't have taken you losing everything to get it?

Eade: Beating myself up, thinking I should be more evolved than I am, blaming myself for where I am, not trusting life.

Pedro: And what untested assumptions are you making about this issue?

Eade: I shouldn't have lost. I shouldn't have taken losing everything. Yeah, just the idea that I shouldn't be where I am, that I shouldn't need this lesson. Not trusting in the process. Not trusting in how much freedom I can gain by really questioning what it would mean to lose everything, really getting okay with that. That's freedom. I'm creating it by not trusting it, not trusting the process that I'm in.

I'm suing my ex, which makes it real for our daughter as well, telling people about it and wanting to tell them. I'm either seeing narcissists when other people talk about their relationships or wanting to protect or prevent people from having to go through this, as if I could prevent or protect someone from their lessons. So, I'm telling other people things that aren't helpful if that's what they need to go through.

Pedro: Let me invite you to take a deep breath and ponder the following question without trying to answer it, Candice. Just ponder and wait for clarity. When you are validating that it shouldn't have taken you to lose everything to get it, what do you miss? What are you not able to see? What is there that you cannot access because you are validating this issue?

Eade: For one thing, I've gained so much. I've gained so much in this divorce for my quality of life, my quality of relationships, my communities, my support systems, my connection with myself. Oh my God, all the attention I gave to my ex and my daughter I can put into my own life now. My own life is flourishing now. I would so much rather have meaningful relationships, and community, and a committed path, and then retirement. So, I'm just totally missing that I've gained everything that I said mattered to me.

I haven't actually lost anything yet. Maybe the attorney fees, but I haven't actually lost anything yet. It's all a mind projection. It's not like he came and took money from me.

It was money that I was supposed to get in the future, and I might still get it. I absolutely haven't lost everything materially. Yes, thinking it, that I've lost everything, it's so wrong. It's just so untrue. I've gained so much more than I've lost.

What am I missing? Just in this moment I'm missing that I'm getting free of codependency. Hallelujah! And it's not like, oh, it's too late. I should have gotten this sooner. There is just none of that. It's like, wow, in this moment I'm at a place where I can get free of this. Wow, what a miracle! I'm so grateful, so profoundly grateful!

Pedro: So how would you live now from this space?

Eade: Much more in the here and now, much less in the past and the future. Yes. More devotion to awareness, less distraction from the world. Just letting this process play itself out and not being engaged, not being involved, having attention on slowing down enough, stopping enough to have moments of awareness throughout the day. Deeper lingering and awareness as it appears, but being able to focus on that, not as the carrot or the Holy Grail, but as an integrated part of my day every day. Taking breaks to just remember there is really no Eade as I project it to be. Taking breaks to dip my toe in the water of awareness in the midst of whatever might be happening and just continue to become more and more comfortable with that, drinking from that source.

In this place right here, right now, in the space, there is something distracting running over here. It's a movie with characters, and plots, and themes, and outcomes, and fear, and projections, and expectations, and anticipations, and all of that. And it's so insignificant. There is not even a temptation to look at it anymore. It is completely boring and untrustworthy. It just is so insignificant.

What's new and fresh and exciting and clear is that none of that is me. Whatever this me is, none of that is actually me. That's just a show that's running. Like there are shows running on Broadway and shows running in London, there is a show running here inside my head that looks like a lawsuit. Just the reminder to keep coming back to what I really want to put my attention on, to get more and more comfortable with just expanding into, settling into. Letting that be that body temperature water to immerse in.

Pedro: So, how valid is the original issue still after this inquiry, zero being nothing and 10 being max? It shouldn't have taken me to lose everything to get it.

Eade: It's a zero.

Pedro: Allow yourself to recognize this space. Deeply relax into it and expand it to corners of your body, every single cell. As you do that, I invite you to do the movement outwards as well. Expand it into absolutely every single space around you and this world, in all directions. This space of clarity, understanding, self-emerging insight, compassion, peace and knowing is home. This home is a space of full alignment, full openness, full curiosity, full connectedness, full availability. And we come back every time we practice IBC, and we make it home, and we live our lives from here rather than from the projected and confused mind.

6

I Feel Like a Nervous Little Girl

Tania: When you validate that you feel very nervous, what images do you see?

Paulette: Okay. I'm feeling it right here. I feel jittery. I see images of people who are like men, men who are just completely wired differently from me. They don't seem to have any personal strife, they think totally differently, so that none of the stuff I say makes sense to them. So that's the figure in my mind that makes me nervous. I see images of disappointment in the man who is in charge of the whole thing, the man who hired me. I see him going, "Oh no, I thought it was going to be way better than this". That sort of awkwardness. I see a bunch of people on the one hand feeling sorry for me and at the same time feeling very impatient. A sense that people want me to leave the room, you know, the sense of like, get out.

Tania: When you see all these images, from 0 to 10, how intense is the feeling of nervousness?

Paulette: Like a 9.

Tania: Okay. So, tell me, who is this Paulette that's nervous? Tell me about her. Who does she turn into when she validates that she is feeling very nervous?

Paulette: She turns into this sort of desperate, small, misunderstood little girl, who is vying for attention and recognition and who just has this sense that she will never get that in her life. She is small.

Tania: Yes. So when this nervous Paulette is there and present, who do others turn into around her?

Paulette: Scary ogres. Scary, dominant men who have no interest in small little Paulette, who have more important things to do, who operate in a different way, who are busy in the real world. People with busy, with real things to do, not interested in Paulette and her little things.

Tania: Yes. And this Paulette that wants that, that feels small, how does she exaggerate things?

Paulette: Well, she exaggerates her own smallness. She exaggerates physically how short she is. I see her as being this little person. She exaggerates the degree to which men don't feel. It's like a super exaggerated form of projected toxic masculinity.

Like a storybook version and an ogre. It's an extreme version of maleness, certainly not one that I associate with any of the men I'm close to. So, she exaggerates that aspect of men. She also brings down her own accomplishments in this world, her own things that she has actually done in quote, the real world. She is a doctor and a mother and directs a nonprofit and makes money and all that, owns her own home, everything. Like that just doesn't exist or is not enough.

Tania: So, tell me about this Paulette, that gets nervous like this, how does she get paralyzed?

Paulette: Yes. It's a form of physical paralysis. I can feel it. It's cold. It's a paralysis of imagination. It's a paralysis of memory. It's a paralysis of not remembering positive conversations with people, of not remembering successful outcomes. It's a paralysis of understanding of the human condition. It's the sort of a paralysis that I can't see that. It feels like the flow of energy, and the flow of inspiration, the flow of knowledge, and understanding, just stops. Certainly, the flow of energy, yes, the flow of energy and creativity.

Tania: And what are the patterns that show up when she gets nervous, when this Paulette, this identity is alive and nervous and exaggerating masculinity and disregard for herself?

Paulette: There is a pattern of wanting other people to come in and help. There is a pattern of saying, "Oh, please, someone". You know, looking for approval, looking for reassurance in conversations with my husband. There is a pattern of not being able to sort this out in the present moment. There is a sense like, okay, I'll get over this later, because I know I've gotten over this before. It will pass, even though right now I'm just paralyzed.

And then patterns of turning other people into ogres, patterns of throwing the baby out with the bath water, a pattern of perfectionism. You know, in those seven talks, there were probably 50 people who gave good grades and three who didn't in one particular talk. And it's like not being able to see the other 47. It's not being able to see that there is something in all of us that seems to be working. That there is something that maybe needs fine-tuning, but I can't even go there because I'm just so paralyzed.

Tania: And what untested assumptions is this Paulette making??

Paulette: Well, she is assuming that what happened in that last experience will happen again. The past becomes the future and then she is trapped. She creates it by seeing herself as so small. There is no confidence. So, she creates it by forgetting the confidence that has been there in the past. She creates it by, well, just by going there, by going into that persona.

She makes these big assumptions that everybody is like that, that everybody has got this sort of toxic masculinity, that everybody is totally out of touch with their feelings, that everybody has got no time for me, that men are just a certain way. You know, the prototype. It's almost like every man is like that. Everybody falls on that side of the curb. Us little girls and women are in this part of the curve and then there is nothing but men. And then everybody else is on that side of toxic masculinity.

Tania: So, take a deep breath and close your eyes and notice when this nervous identity is alive, and you create this construct. What is the little girl missing then? Don't think with your mind, just open up and wait for insight. Look. Look at her. Look at all the things she feels and thinks and assumes and exaggerates and paralyzes. What is she missing?

Paulette: Yeah. She is missing... You know, she is missing the connection that she has already established with the leader of the group. I've met with him twice and had great conversations and he is like, "When are we going to do this?" She is also missing the hundreds and hundreds of hours of time spent in this domain with people who, when they show who they really are, it makes you realize that we are all the same. Missing that suffering is such a pervasive problem. Chronic stress is such a pervasive problem that no one is immune to.

I am missing my own capacity to connect. I miss the scenarios in which I actually do very well. I miss that, that's my wheelhouse. That's not a problem. I miss that failure, even if it were to come back, it's not the end of it all. It's becoming friends with failure and all that the failure has to show me.

What I'm missing is awareness. What I'm missing in that space is that everything that comes to me when I'm in the mind is all a gift for real. It's not just lip service, It's real. And it's all for me. What I'm really missing is that no matter what the outcome, it's all for me. For my growth, for my learning. For my joy!

Tania: So feel that right now in your body and just look at that little nervous one and just say, "I see you. Thank you". And like a soap bubble, you can pop this limiting vision of her. I see you. Thank you. Pop! And relax into this awareness. And notice, how would you move now? How would you live your life from this awareness?

Paulette: It's funny, the words, "Welcome home" just keep popping into my mind. Welcome home. Welcome home! That's what I would feel like! It's a sense of receiving them, of welcoming them to my inner home. There is a sense of receiving these people who not long ago I was rejecting as toxic males. It's not a grandiose, like, welcome to me. It's more like in my mind, there is a deep welcoming like a valued guest in my house kind of thing.

Tania: So, what becomes now new, fresh, or even exciting that was not there before this inquiry?

Paulette: It's calming. It's an exciting calmness. It's a calmness and grounded-ness that's oddly fresh and exciting. The energy itself isn't one of excitement. It's an energy of grounded-ness, and openness, and warmth, and joy, and understanding and deep knowing.

Tania: So breathe, stay there and expand that for a moment. Let it just unfold like a wrinkly piece of silk that's just extended and slowly through the crown of her head, all the way to the tips of your fingers and toes and your organs and beyond.

Paulette: Yes.

Tania: So, what's the clear opportunity now? If the little one or the nervous one shows up again, what is the opportunity? What is the opportunity from this place?

Paulette: To receive the little nervous one with deep receptive energy. It's receiving her, welcoming her home. It feels clear. It makes sense. And as much as I really see that I'm not that, there is a place that's still, that. There is a place where she still exists in discovery. And that's not to be rejected.

Tania: Of course, she is innocent.

Paulette: Yes, so innocent.

Tania: So, what is a clear next step for you, if any?

Paulette: I recorded myself giving a talk yesterday, just on my computer and I had the thought about sending it out for feedback. Now I'm pretty sure I will. And I'll be very directive in that and say, "What is it about this that I could make more? Where is it that the little girl energy is coming through? And what practical steps can I take to not come from that place?" So, it makes sense to talk to somebody who is a mentor. I can have a mentorship conversation with him. I think that would be helpful.

Tania: And what makes you think that he can hear the little girl better than you from this place?

Paulette: I don't know if he can. I think showing up for him just saying, "Can you listen to this and tell me what you think?" Being really open and grounded about that I think would help me just to dissect it, and be with it, and be vulnerable.

Tania: And I'm asking you now to really check, Paulette. Is this part of the little girl? Because her pattern is to ask for help.

Paulette: Yes. That's true. That is true, isn't it? Daddy number two. Touché. Yeah. Yeah. Good, good. Good pick up.

Tania: So, what's left? Tell me what's going on right now. What's left? You started at a nine and then you got to a very beautiful space. And then this next step you said to ask for feedback and then something got activated again. So, what's left there? What's going on there in your body? What number would you say you are at in regard to this nervousness now?

Paulette: Four or five, say five.

Tania: So, let's look at the five and see what's going on there. What's left in the form of an image, sensation, thought, behind this five?

Paulette: A thought that just came up is I need other people to help me. Yeah. Other people or a corollary, other people know better than I do. I had the same thought about you today, I was like, "Oh, this timing is great with Tania. She can help me today".

Tania: Right. So tell me about that person? Who is that? I need other people to help me.

Paulette: It's obviously implicit, if I'm asking people to help, it's because other people should know better. It's putting wisdom or some kind or power outside.

Tania: Can you feel that movement of energy in your body? Describe it to me.

Paulette: So, I think the earlier one felt more up here in head. This feels like a constriction in my upper abdomen, a tightening in the sort of upper area of the belly. It's the part of me that wants to abdicate my own intuition, and power, and understanding, and voice, to an outside consultant, an outside expert. So, if I'm running a business and I can't figure it out, I'm like, "Okay, let's call the consultants in, tell us what's going on."

Tania: And what does she get out of giving her power away?

Paulette: Connection. A lot of the things I do are in the name of connection. It's the big one for me. The sense of connection. And it feels like a very female energy, like connecting over the parts of me that are deficient. It's like giving something away, exaggerating something in me to form a connection with somebody else.

And the nuance that just came into my mind was that I only do this with certain people, you know, I do this with certain people. I can really distinctly think of some friends as friends that I do that bend-over thing. So, it's more with certain people.

Tania: So, what is the core pattern of this aspect, of this kind of identity? I need people's help because they know better than me, while giving away your power.

Paulette: So by doing that, there is a bit of flattery to the other person, and that would give me more connection. They are more likely to go, "Oh no, you are super great, Paulette". So it's almost transactional in that way. I just really flatter them, and then they are more likely to reassure me or speak highly of me. It's a false lure actually, a form of manipulation. It's not always, but it really happens when

I'm feeling like this nervous little girl. When I'm feeling nervous, when I'm feeling nervous about something coming up, or I'm sort of stuck on a failure, stuck on a problem at work, a case that I missed at work, or an outcome in the medical world that didn't happen the way I wanted it to. When I get in that place, that's where this habit comes up the most. It's a form of grasping.

It's a grasping that says, I don't know how to do this by myself, and it's also about connection. It's like I've got to connect now because I need that drug to make me feel better and how best to connect than to flatter the other person first. Yeah, sort of the two combined, which is crazy.

Tania: So, what does she miss? What does this part of you miss when she wants connection this way?

Paulette: Well, you know, it's a little bit of that going on with these people. I actually want connection from these apparently toxic males. There is part of that becomes the example of the Southern belle walking into this room of men saying, "Please help me", you know? "Be so kind as to listen to me please", you know? And in those moments, that's when I start thinking, okay, what am I going to wear? How is that going to look? I've got to get my makeup done. What's my hair going to look like? Like just total female, female, female.

Tania: So what does she miss? This damsel in distress?

Paulette: Yes, this damsel in distress. She misses that she is already connected enough as it is. She misses that she can do this on her own. There is a speed element to this too, Tania, like it has to happen now. So she misses that if she slows it down, this will settle itself whole. She misses that.

Tania: Feel that for a moment. Feel that and breathe that in your body and your belly.

Tania: Does that land in your belly?

Paulette: Yeah. Yeah. And you know, right away I get images of things I've accomplished completely by myself. Like, nobody helped me get into medical school. Nobody helped me sort out my son. That was all me. In the end, really the big things I've ever done have come very much from a sense of that inner voice and light going, okay, do this thing. It's time to do this thing. Yeah, I can really find that.

Tania: Do you feel that? Yeah, can you see that one? Feel that wise, aware, clear problem-solver.

Paulette: Yeah. I'm like one of the better problem-solvers that I know of in this world.

Tania: So, what's new, fresh and exciting now? How would she live this moment?

Paulette: Yeah. I mean, she would show up as an adult. She just shows up as the one who has lived the story that

I'm actually telling, which is that life kicks our butt and even when we get outward success, it doesn't mean that we will be inwardly successful. And that's my story. And so I've traveled to this place and that place and done this thing and this thing and this thing because I wanted to start figuring this out and here I am. And if you want to hear it, here it is. It's like sharing the story more. It's like sharing more about my adventure. I've been dispatched to go think about this stuff and I'm coming back and here it is guys. This is what I found out. Do you want to hear it?

Tania: How does it feel?

Paulette: It just feels like me. It just feels energetic and happy. There is almost a humor in it. Like all this stuff, this whole dream, this whole thing. It's like it's joy! Life is a comedy, not a tragedy. And look at the shit show anyways! It's the reflection of the comedic aspects of it. And so, there is an energy to it that's just a return to that energy in me that I know I have when I'm connected, just a return to that.

Tania: Yeah. So let's check in with that five. Where are you now?

Paulette: It's like a two, three.

Tania: Okay.

Paulette: Three.

Tania: Let's see what's left.

Paulette: I still have this place of like, I need his. I need his. I need his approval.

Tania: And how do you validate that?

Paulette: Yeah, it's a magnet. It's a magnet and it's the final doubt for me. Going through this, you are like walking through the forest on your own. You've done all this and there is this little stick right before you get in and you trip. It's the nagging little place that's like, are you sure? Really? Are you really so sure that you are okay? It's this doubting, place.

Tania: And where does doubt live in your body?

Paulette: It's a falling in my belly. It's like a set of tired, falling feeling, just a like the final straw, the nail in the casket. But like, no, no, you are just fooling yourself. It's just shit. It's just all crap. You are not onto something here.

Tania: Yes. So, who do you turn into, Paulette, when you completely receive this energy?

Paulette: Yes, the skeptic, the sarcastic skeptic. I turn into that. You know, I turn into that man who is just like this crock of shit, you know, bullshit. What the hell? What are you talking about? Nah! Yeah, I turn into him. I turn into that skeptical, dark person. It's a darkness, but it's not like a deep dark night of the soul kind of darkness. It's just like a shallow darkness. You know what I mean? It's not the kind of darkness that comes with benefits. It's more like a darkness coming from a toxic fume that just takes away awareness, takes away joy, takes away life. But not harshly enough to really bring you to back to your knees.

Tania: Who do others turn into?

Paulette: They turn into people that are all full of shit. They turn into the bottom line, you know, where's the money? What are the numbers here? He is conservative politically. He is money oriented. He thinks that strength is in economic power. He thinks that being really pessimistic will get you somewhere. There is no soft underbelly. Taking joy in grading people poorly.

Tania: So how do you exaggerate, paralyze, or disconnect? How do you do that?

Paulette: Yeah, I do it by thinking poorly about other people, by seeing people for their faults, for their worst aspects. I disconnect by thinking that everybody else is like that. So, in that moment, maybe there is one guy I'm projecting all of this on, and then you've got like four dudes who are like, "Okay, tell me more". And I'm like, "No, no, I'm not interested in you. I'm interested in the one over here that is not interested in me". I'm more interested in the one who is cynical, yeah, cynical, more than skeptical. So, I exaggerate by thinking the whole world is like that.

I exaggerate by saying that men are all like that. All men are like that, really. And that all women are weak, and all men are like that, projecting all of that onto people. That's power. That's how it is. And it's completely not accessing the part of me that just adores people.

Tania: So what do you miss? What do you throw away in that moment?

Paulette: When I turn into the cynic, I throw away my own experience of inner connection and alignment. The connection even with my mom. It was so close, the connection to music and nature and all that. Threw away all of that. Threw away the goodies. I notice I do that. In particular, I've got this one friend in town, and I do that to her. I can feel from the bottom of my boots to my top of my head what it is just to be me in that moment in alignment without throwing away the goods. A deep sense of containment.

Tania: Yeah. And this containment, Paulette, this containment, this experience that you are just telling me right now in your body, what is it affording you more than anything if you don't think of anyone else except yourself?

Paulette: Yeah, joy. It's the source of joy. It's the source of... Yeah, joy!

Tania: Yeah. So breathe that, expand that, that joy. Does it feel aligned?

Paulette: Very much. Yeah. Yeah.

Tania: So, you were at a two or three, where do you feel now in this alignment, in this joy? Check in from the alignment, from the joy.

Paulette: Yeah, zero. Yeah.

Tania: Recognize it. Breathe it. Expand it. Let it ripple your brain, your cells, your heart. Feel how you have this already. It's already yours. You did not create it, you just uncovered something that was behind the noise already.

Paulette: Yeah, it's really good. Yeah. It's like a return to yourself. I just feel reconnected to myself, just reconnected to source, energy, reconnected to God, to nature. That being, that being-ness, reconnection to being-ness, just reconnection to the unconditional. Thank you.

7

I Want to Stop Overthinking Things

Carmen: Well, my goal is to **stop overthinking things**. You know, very succinctly put.

Pedro: Okay. So you overthink things too much. That is the issue?

Carmen: Yes, absolutely.

Pedro: And how valid is this issue on a scale of 1 to 10?

Carmen: Oh, I would say I'm definitely a 10 on that one.

Pedro: So, you overthink too much, Carmen. How do you validate this? What's your proof? How do you make this issue a real thing for yourself, that you overthink too much?

Carmen: I look at all sorts of possibilities. I make lists. I do contingency plans. I think of the good, the bad, and the ugly. I compare to the past. I project into the future. You know, this lovely imagination of how things might turn out or not. I can almost feel the thinking spinning inside my head. Yeah. I get into a lot of detail. I try and project outcomes. I do, oh my gosh, I do lists. Yes, just lots of lists of details and what ifs. I look at lessons learned in the past, which are hopeful, but I think I frame a lot of how I don't want things to work out and really stress out about this. And so, I look at past experiences and look at the good, the bad, the ugly, and then really use those three for framing future thoughts or future plans, and this is exhausting! Constantly thinking of wanting to avoid pain points that I had in the past.

Pedro: When you are validating that you overthink too much, who do you turn into in your mind? When your mind is validating, insisting, convincing yourself that you overthink too much, who do you turn into?

Carmen: I think in part I turn into somebody who has to get it right out of the gates. I turn into somebody who has all the pieces already figured out in my mind and then suffer because life does not cooperate with my plan. I turn into somebody who is afraid of repeating past errors. You know what, that's a good one. I turn into somebody who is always really worried of repeating past errors. This somehow is a big worry for me, I need to have learned. Otherwise, the pain has been a waste of time. If there wasn't a lesson learned, then what's the point?

Pedro: And who do others turn into? So, for example, who shows up in your mind when you are validating that you overthink too much? Who shows up and who do they turn into?

Carmen: People that have something great going on, and then I compare myself with them. So, others turn into successful people, and they turn into people that have everything figured out. Others turn into people who are nailing it. And then the comparison comes in. You know, I've got to get it right. I've got to nail it. They are impressive. Others are impressive, I would say this is a big one, actually. They turn into people who are getting it right, but I don't actually dig into how they got there. It's like a snapshot. So, it's not a movie reel. It's a snapshot. And they are getting it right in the snapshot.

Pedro: So, when you are validating that you overthink too much, how are you exaggerating? How do you disconnect or freeze when you are convincing yourself, pedalling this idea that you overthink too much? How do you exaggerate, disconnect, or freeze?

Carmen: Well, I disconnect because I'm very in my head and I'm very busy being analytical. So yes, I disconnect from any indicators in the body. I exaggerate in needing to have it all sorted out before I even start, and I exaggerate in the projections of possible outcomes. I think I might also exaggerate in the notion of having an exit plan with all the possible contingency details sorted out. So, I think there is an exaggeration of scope, oh, and an exaggeration of detail.

And I freeze into a spin cycle. I freeze into this sort of hyperloop instead of just being calm and letting something other than my thinking have a space.

Pedro: And when you are validating that you overthink too much, what is repetitive? What's cyclical? What patterns show up for you?

Carmen: It's definitely a pattern to looking into what's happened in the past, and then projecting into the future how that needs to play out or not play out. It's sort of this recipe of mine, I guess is the pattern. Also, a pattern is actually just getting bogged down in the details. Instead of feeling where the most excitement lies, which could be a great indicator for me I'm in this pattern of analysis, and then I try and choose based this analysis I'm doing. I develop a concept, I flush through a little bit of the good, the bad, the ugly, and then I move on to the next concept and I flush through the good, the bad, the ugly, and then I move on to the next one, and so on. And so that is a pattern, a cycle, and repetitive, that I don't get out from. I don't seem to ever actually get out of the loop.

Pedro: So, when you are exaggerating, disconnecting, freezing, when you are in the loop, what untested assumptions are you making?

Carmen: Well, I can apply this thought method to anything and everything forever and have zero progress, zero outcome. Yes. So it's not helpful. It's only helpful for some key markers, and then it just becomes debilitating actually.

So I cause this issue for myself in terms of the detail that I get into. Yeah. And it's all imagined anyway because it's just about projections and thoughts popping into the screen of the future which may have zero basis in reality. So really I am creating it for myself by projecting something that is contrived as if it was real. Yes. So, it's the too many details and the projecting how I create this for myself.

Pedro: And what assumptions do you make of others?

Carmen: Well, I make assumptions about my existing business partner, and because we are talking about doing something new, I have thrown out all sorts of ideas at him and doing the same for him that I do for myself. And then I convince others about what's exciting about one project and then I convince them about what's exciting about a different project, and repeat, and repeat. Not actually taking any action at all. I'm just in an endless loop thinking these different options. And then this actually impedes action for him because he gets caught up with me in my spin cycle.

Pedro: So, let me invite you to take a deep breath, close your eyes and ponder the following question Carmen, without trying to answer it, just ponder the question and wait for insight. When you are validating that you overthink too much, when this assumption, this issue is driving your perception, your mind, your actions, what do you miss? What are you not able to see when you are being driven by this assumption that you overthink too much? Don't try to come up with an answer. Just notice and wait for insight. What do you miss? What are you not able to see?

Carmen: [Prolonged pause] I'm not able to see what's already immediately available to me, there and with ease. I'm projecting and I'm not able to notice what's right in front of me. I'm not able to notice what I could do in a facilitated manner, that what I could start with ease that hits a bunch of targets I'm not able to notice that I can just start without all the details. I don't need to have all the answers. Also, I'm not able to notice how I won't be able to take action if I keep in that mind loop, because it's just a never ending loop without action.

Also, I'm not able to notice that once I start something or take action on something, then I can actually apply this very powerful and efficient thinking to what is *actually* unfolding in real life as opposed to what I am *projecting* that potentially, possibly, may unfold. So, I can actually apply my thinking practically and constructively instead of hypothetically. Yes, I like that one. I really like that. Oh my gosh, all this thinking and all this detail I get into, which can also be very good. It can be very good applied in the right way and it's only debilitating applied in the wrong way! So, I just need to switch what it is that I'm applying to. That's what I need! Yeah!

Pedro: I see, so how would you live your life now without validating that you overthink too much? Just close your eyes and notice your life. What can you see now about your life? How do you live your life without validating, I overthink too much?

Carmen: I'm catching myself in this, almost a reactive panic. Like I'm having this total sensation of this reactive panic of not being able to let go the loop. I can't let go of the loop. It's like traveling up to my head, like some weird thing that I've got to hang on to. But living without that, I could actually say, okay, what do I really feel? What do I actually *feel*? And then it's like I don't trust my feelings enough and my head has to dominate.

So, living, I would live my life just being calmer of mind, allowing myself to feel and then take a step from that place of feeling and not from the space of a contriving loop. I like that, and then one step, and then the next step, and then the next step, instead of having this whole projection from start to finish and everything in between. Yeah, it's just moving forward and stopping the mind. I would live outside of my head, feel.

Pedro: So, let this one sink in for a bit. Take a deep breath and allow yourself to really feel this next step, breathing, pause, expansion, this completion and then the next step, action. And then breathing, noticing, expansion, completion. And then again, next step, the same. Just sit in that clarity. And from this space, Carmen, consider the question, what is the worst that would happen if you were to completely let go of this pattern of thinking too much, of this loop? What would you lose? What is the worst that would actually happen if you were to completely let go of it, entirely, 100%?

Carmen: [Prolonged pause] You know, I have to almost

smile to myself because I can't actually think of anything that would be a problem!

Pedro: Surprise! And look for it. Honestly, I mean, look for it. The clarity and the transformation come from the internal, grounded evidence that we find when we are doing inquiry. So, go for it, look for it. What is the worst possible outcome? What are we so afraid, so petrified of if we let go? What is the worst possible outcome?

Carmen: Yeah. It's like the worst outcome I can come up with is I pick something and either I didn't like it as much as I thought, or it didn't turn out as much as I thought, and I could then just stop doing it. No loss! I could transfer it to somebody else. I could sell it. I know I have tons of resources and then I can successfully deal with the consequences of anything that comes my way. I have experience, I have tools, I have knowledge, I have resources, I have support. Yes, the worst outcome actually doesn't exist! It about the driving not about the destination! It has always been about, oh, the driving. I really like the sense of unfolding when the focus is on the process and not in the results. Oh my gosh, it's exciting! It's interesting. There is actually even a profound lightness to it because I am noticing that I am actually not driving. The Universe is Driving! Oh gosh, I love it! Oh my gosh! That just so nailed it! It's like this enclosed, insular capsule of "shut up, I'm driving" from the Universe letting go of my shitty spin cycle. Oh my gosh, I love the illustration of that. Oh gosh! Yes!

Pedro: So how would you live your life now actually having a conversation with the universe while driving?

Carmen: Yeah. It would be freeing and enlightening, and it would be beautifully stimulating from a good input versus this recycled small thought. It would be more fun. I would live my life having fun and trusting in the unfolding.

Pedro: Could you find clear, concrete examples of how you are actually already doing that in some areas in your life? How you are actually allowing the Universe to drive in some areas already.

Carmen: Wow. Funny enough, I did it twice with two business start-ups a decade ago where we just picked and ran with it and let it unfold and both turned out great. And then funny enough, for the first time in my life, I'm actually doing it in a personal relationship! Actually, right at the outset we talked, I said, "Let's let things unfold, not prescribe anything or put a timeframe around things or label things." And it's been going great.

So yes! I am actually doing it! I'm doing it already! That's so funny. And I actually said, "let's let things unfold" which is absolutely crazy for me to do. And this feeling has continued to carry forward in a great way and now different conversations arise, and none of it is scripted. All of it has just been unfolding and it has been a great ride.

Pedro: So, what is now new, fresh, exciting, or clear that was not there before this inquiry?

Carmen: Honestly, even the fact that I'm already doing it was not clear to me. So, the knowing that I actually can do it is tremendously powerful. I am amazed at how easy it has been with this partner and that's exciting. To apply the same thing, and how easy it can be to everything else in my life, to just let something unfold and then apply the thinking when it is actually needed in the moment.

What totally just went poof for me was, that what's new and fresh and exciting is that the power is actually in the unfolding not in the controlling. That's really where the power is. It's just taking a step, and then the next, and then the next, and letting it unfold. There is no power in overthinking, that's actually completely debilitating. Yeah, so I love it. I love it. The power is in the driving, in the step by step, and in the unfolding.

Pedro: So how is this issue actually an opportunity? I overthink too much?

Carmen: It's an opportunity to set aside that thinking. That super detailed thinking when I actually need to apply it to either a problem or to a creative something. That's when I could get into all this detail that I'm so good at machinating. So, yes, it's an opportunity to use it when the time is right. There it is, but not to drive the decision making myself. Yes.

Pedro: What do you see as specific and concrete next steps?

Carmen: I'm going to draw a cartoon as a reminder, like literally. So, I'm going to put it up in my office to help me notice when I get back into that, if and when I get back into that mindset. And then when something arises, I'm going to write down the thought and then I'm going to just sit with it, and do nothing, and actually see, yes, just open up and listen to the Universe. There is all this open space, and there is often very little traffic in a wide, expansive Universe. So it's like me and the universal road, and the open space, and my mind has a chance to be more open or be freer somehow.

Pedro: So on a scale of 0 being nothing and 10 being max, how valid is I overthink too much?

Carmen: I can comfortably feel that it's a zero. I have completely redirected where that thinking needs to go. Yes, where that thinking serves and where it doesn't.

Pedro: So that statement in itself "I overthink too much" is not valid at all now and all the energy has moved into what is now of service to you, and clarity to you.

Carmen: Yes, totally, totally. I actually completely feel it in my body.

8

I Can't Breathe at Night

John: I am at a 10 right now.

Tania: How are these emotions and these images showing up for you? Tell me. Empty your mind as to what shows up at night when you are feeling like you cannot breathe.

John: Yes. So I wake up at night because I can't breathe and my mind immediately goes into what's wrong with me? There is like a dialogue, like a war going on inside of me between me and the victim. You know, what's wrong with me? Why is this happening? Why don't I feel better? Am I always going to feel like this? And along with that come images of when I was a child, I had asthma and allergies and they were really bad. I used to get allergy shots three times a week and I had an inhaler and I had a machine for emergencies. If my throat closed up, they put me on machine. I go right back there, and I feel like I go right back there, and I also project it forward. So, I feel like that's the trajectory that I'm on. Like I started here and that's where

I'm headed again. It's just going to get worse and it's not going to get figured out and it's not going to get better.

And then at the same time, the other voice that goes to war with this is like: No, that's not the problem. The problem is you are living in the wrong place. You should've never agreed to this. You are so stupid. You are so foolish. Why did you agree to live on the East Coast and in the Mid-Atlantic, and didn't you know it was like full of allergies and you have to get out of here? It's like these two voices are screaming at me and screaming at each other, and I'm caught in the middle feeling just totally overwhelmed, overwhelmed, numb, emotionally shut down, wired. It's like the middle of the night and I'm totally wired up for no reason. Well, except that there is a war going on inside of me.

Tania: So that's three voices. Okay, let's name them. Let's give them a name to these identities.

John: There is the sick one.

Tania: The sick one that is like a poor victim.

John: Yeah. Yup. Then voice number two is like an authority figure. This one, he steps in and he is like, "No, all that's wrong. You messed this up, but you know. You made some bad decisions, but..." So, he is the... He is not a judge, but he is like... He is like the CEO.

Tania: And then the third one?

John Right. The third one is the one I was thinking of as me. He can't stand the... He gets overwhelmed by all the noise and he numbs out, yeah. Yeah. He numbs out and then you know he is with me during the day too!

Tania: Numbing you out during the day.

John: Yeah, yeah. I have an hour of free time and you know, it's like I could play guitar, or I could do inquiry and instead I watch a movie.

Tania: Okay. So now I want you to look at the three. You have them? Okay. Tell me who does your partner turn into for each of the three?

John: Yeah. So for the CEO, she is a villain. She is the head of the company that this company is at war with. And for the victim, she becomes just a bad caretaker. She gets frustrated. She gets frustrated that she can't do more. She doesn't know what to do. And then she just can't deal. She becomes a bad caretaker and it's really painful for me. For the checked-out one, she is clueless. She just doesn't know how I'm feeling, and she is... She is the one who is off doing the thing that I want to do, and she is living her life and she is enjoying it and she has no idea what's going on over here.

Tania: So, for the three of them, I want you to now tell me what living in your previous location is for each of them.

John: Yeah. I think we started with the CEO before. Let's keep him as number one. He is the loudest. For him this location is the place for John to shine, for John to make a difference, to inspire others and to be inspired and to really, to be a hero. For the victim, this is a place to recuperate. It has got sun, it has got dry air, doesn't have mold, or you know, pollens. It's like, it's warm, it's dry, it has got that salty ocean breeze. It's just the place that he wants to go to feel better. It's the perfect place, actually. It's the perfect combination of dry and warm and salt for the sinuses. It's like it's Avalon.

Tania: Yeah. And for the checked-out one?

John: I think the checked-out one feels… He just feels safe there. There are safe people there. There are a lot of people, even some of my students, people that I can be vulnerable with, and I don't have to put on a false front with about how I'm feeling or how I'm doing, where he can just… He feels safe to just let his guard down.

Tania: Okay. We are holding a lot here. We are holding all the pieces. So now let's look at how these three characters, the victim, the CEO, and the checked-out one, how do they exaggerate about the whole situation?

John: Yeah. So for my partner, yeah, it's a big exaggeration. She is really struggling. I make it sound like it's super easy for her to be there, and it's not. She is struggling with work life balance. She is struggling with changing the mission of her company and keeping it meaningful. And you know, this week she asked me to come and teach to her staff. But it's not the same. I project everything was amazing in the old location, but it wasn't all heroic, far from it, quite the opposite. It took a lot of work to get there. And I imagine if I had stayed or if I went back – and I went back to work or even another school – that it would be like that every year, that it would be a real struggle and that there would be times of me feeling heroic, and there would be times of me just wondering what the heck I was doing down there and wondering if it mattered and if, you know all of it, from the highest high to the lowest low.

Tania: Yeah. So how is the victim exaggerating?

John: He is right there. He is like... It's like when the doctor hits your knee with that thing. It's just like he is just right... He is right there ready to jump into the drama.

Tania: Yeah. Let's look at that. Let's look at the patterns of these. Look at the pattern of the checked-out one. Is he familiar?

John: Oh yes, very. One of the big things about him is he waits until he feels better. So it's kind of like, you know, exercise, diet, work. He is waiting. He is waiting until he feels better as if there were no steps. I'm not saying that like, whatever. There is a recovery, and there is a reality to not feeling well, but the pattern with him is, nope, there is nothing that can be done right now. Shove everything. You've got to clear the plate, nothing is getting through, and when we feel better, then we'll start reengaging with life. But until then, no, I'm stepping out, just stepping out.

Tania: And how does the CEO feel about that? Is he okay with that pattern?

John: No.

Tania: How does he react?

John: Big time, shame. Big time shame him, big time. What the heck is wrong with you? Like, do you know that you are 47 now. Like how much longer are you going to wait? Just on and on, like, get up off your ass. And then he goes into like starving people in Africa and people in war torn countries, and like what a cake walk I have and how my problems are nothing. And snap out of it. You are pathetic.

Tania: Then in comes the...

John: Victim. I just can't do... I just can't do it. I just can't do it. It's too much. I can't do it.

Tania: So can you see, John, how they co-create together, how they co-create the whole experience?

John: Yes.

Tania: There are three key movements, resistance- the checked-out one, shaming- the CEO and what's the third with the victim?

John: The word that comes to mind, but not in a spiritual sense is surrender, just giving up.

Tania: Yeah, for me that's powerlessness.

John: Powerlessness. Yeah. That's it, hopeless and powerless. And the more hopeless and the more powerless, the more shame and then the more checked out.

Tania: Of course, they need each other to survive, the three of them. Okay. So now can you see, John, that there is an awareness? There is one that watches the three.

John: Yes. And even when I talk about how reactive I am right now, and maybe I am or maybe I mostly am, I still have these occasional moments where I see it so clearly and I... not as clearly as we've just arrived at here, but where I marvel at these characters, specifically the CEO and the victim.

Tania: Yes. I want you to take a breath and to just, from this space of the one that watches the three, to really notice, to really look at what they are missing. What are they not able to see? Take your time to look for the answer with your mind. Just hold these innocent, innocent constructs that you've built for the purpose of surviving. You see them. Yeah, I see you. What are they missing?

John: The first thing that I noticed is, this is painful. I don't know why. The first thing I notice is that people are interested in me. I don't know how else to say it. When I drop my son off at school, when I go to the coffee shop, when I... There was this period of time in LA where I was depressed, and I just felt like I was invisible for a while. This is like the opposite. This is like everyone wants to know who I am and what I'm doing. It's really interesting and not at all how I'm perceiving my life, or how I'm perceiving others. There is a serious disconnect there. I am missing that I'm okay. I'm okay. I really am okay. It is possible that I'm better than I think I am. I'm not hooked up to a breathing machine and I'm not getting shots multiple times a week. And when I look at it, I was okay then too. I was okay, actually. And now it's like, I'm just really okay.

Tania: Yeah.

John: I'm noticing how much I've really enjoyed having some time, some quiet time alone in the last few weeks while feeling sick. I was really overstimulated when I left our last home, really overstimulated. I was wired big time, and it has been nice to have some time to be quiet and still and to have no agenda. Like I cleared my plate, really cleared my plate for the surgery and for two weeks after, and ever since I've kept more time just to have downtime and it has been really nice, a real gift.

Tania: Yeah. So how would you live your life now without validating these three innocent identities, without giving them so much weight? How would you live?

John: With real ease. Real ease about things. It reminded me of my previous place, actually. Once I had my routine there, there was a kind of ease to it. And I'm seeing that here too. That's taking little moments here to really, really notice and feel the cold air on my skin, just the ease of walking my son to school.

I would definitely be a lot more appreciative of my partner, of how hard she is working and how hard she is trying to support me in her way in this time. I would be happy for her too. She was a little lost in back then and before, after having our son too. She was so in love with him, and it was also really hard for her to not throw herself into work. So I'm rarely seeing how it's good to see her... It's good to see her connected in a way that hasn't been in a while. I'm appreciative of that and grateful for her and for us. And for our son, that he sees that she is doing something that's meaningful to her. That's great.

The checked-out one. I don't know if I mentioned this, but he is always in a hurry. He is in a hurry to do nothing, always. It's so crazy. He is in like just a hurry to get home. And then when he is home, it's like he is in a hurry to eat and then he is in a hurry to get to Netflix, and that he is in a hurry to take out the trash so that he can be in a... It's like, wow.

And you know, I just notice like taking my time without validating these identities. There is a lot more space in my day. There is a lot less hurry. But space is a good word.

Tania: And what's new, fresh, and exciting about that space, about the slowness?

John: It's so... It's very sweet. There was this... I remember I went outside, and I had so many things to do. I had to water the plants and I had to clean the skimmers in the pool, and I had to take the trash out. There was just like this crazy list of things to do. I did all of them, and I enjoyed them so much and I came back inside, and it was like, I still had 15 minutes to eat. It was so cool. I wasn't rushing through them to get to the next one, to get to the food, to get back to the class. It was like I was just so present with what I was doing, and I see the opportunity for that in my life right now. Like it's not... My schedule is not heavy right now. There are things in it, but it's not heavy. And I see a way in which I'm really just kind of flowing through it during this period where I'm not feeling maybe 100%. And it feels so kind and so... It feels like a huge gift. It feels like a huge gift and actually, it feels like it's exactly what I need.

Tania: So take a moment to breathe that awareness, that noticing and expand that into your every cell of your body, to the crown of your head, in your arms, in your fingers, in your legs, in your toes and your lungs, in your sinuses. Just let that gently spread. So, where do you feel right now from 0 to 10? You started at a 10.

John There was a moment of zero, and what came up for me was that that can't be a zero because this is too old, that there is no way that that was a zero. And it's going to take a lot more work.

Tania: So, who is that identity?

John: That's the checked-out guy. Yeah. He doesn't want to do it. He doesn't want to do the work. He doesn't want to get to Zero.

Tania: Yes, so what does he believe will happen if he gets to Zero?

John: He dies.

Tania: And what is he missing?

John: He thinks that if he dies then he can't protect me.

Tania: Just take that in. Take that in. It's so sweet. He has supported you so long. He has helped you survive stuff, right?

John: Before I found out that I had celiac disease, there was a time where I was really sick, and no one could figure out what's wrong with me. I just thought it was going to die, and I wanted to sometimes. He was the one that kept me going, just get through, just get through the day, you know, just get through whatever it takes. Whatever it takes, just get through the day and maybe tomorrow will be better. But for him, tomorrow never comes. He is always thinking tomorrow, but I get the kindness in that. I really do.

Tania: Sure. And from the one that watches him, what is he missing, John?

John: What's coming up for me is just that nobody is going to die, I mean really, I mean, even if I die. Like that makes sense. Like he is missing that... He's missing that I'm missing life. I'm missing out on a big part of life. I'm missing out on joy and sorrow and heartbreak and laughter. The biggest thing I'm missing out on is just the mystery and the unknown, and that anything could happen and does. People just decide to move somewhere else one day and you know, he is missing that anything could happen. And that when things happen, sometimes they hurt and sometimes they are great and sometimes they are both and whatever, but that it's all life. And when he is running the show that, you know, we are missing a big part of life.

Tania: So, if you don't validate him, how would you live now?

John: If I'm not validating him, it's just... It's a hero's journey. It's an adventure walking up the stairs. I don't know what's going to happen. I don't know who's going to be there. I don't know what's going to happen.

Tania: And is that fresh and exciting?

John: Oh, it's amazing. It's amazing, absolutely amazing.

Tania: So, feel that amazingness.

John: Yes.

Tania: Of every moment.

John: Of every moment. Yeah. Look at this moment.

Tania: This is like… You know how cats watch things?

John: Yes.

Tania: Like with their whole bodies. Their eyes cannot be wider. It's so sweet. Just the presence of, what's going to happen now?

John: Yeah. That's totally it. What actually came up for me as you were saying that was a dog I used to have. He just loved the tennis ball, just loved it. Every time I picked it up, I must've picked up the tennis ball 100 million times, every single time, is he going to throw it? Is he going to drop it? Is he going to hide it? Anything could happen. Oh my, this is amazing. He is holding it. It's right there in front of me.

Tania: How does it feel for you right now? Take a breath. Just check in.

John: Very warm, very calm. Rushing is the furthest thing from my mind right now. I feel very connected to my body. Just full of gratitude for, especially the checke- out one, really all of them, but especially that checked out one. So much gratitude. I mean, my God, he works so hard. He works so hard and he just … the amount of fear that he is holding, just the degree to which he will go to try to keep me safe. I mean, it's just... That's unconditional love.

Tania: And can you also just feel the loving presence of the one that watches him?

John: Yeah. Yeah. I think when I say that, that's where it's coming from, because when we first named him, I was confused. I was like, no, no, that's me. And then as we started to separate him, there was like a real revelation. Oh, I feel really good. Thank you so much, Tania. I feel like I could drift off into the most peaceful sleep that I've had since before my surgery.

Tania: Thank you, John.

John: Tania, thank you.

IBC Results

IBC has been tested and offered in two distinct environments with extraordinary results. The first one is the **personal** dimension though coaching and training for self-practice where we have worked with countless individuals interested in substantially improving their lives. The second environment of applicability for IBC has been **organizational** settings where we have been supporting dozens of companies in the development of leaders and high-performing teams.

In this section of the book, we will present experiential results from individuals in the form of relevant testimonials. You can find many more on our website. Additionally, we will present a summary of the results from our corporate evaluations.

If you are a leader in an organization and would like to learn more about IBC and its applications with teams, we would be happy to connect you to other leaders that have brought IBC to their organizations. You can find our evaluation details in our Organizational Results White Paper on our website as well. Feel free to visit **innerland.com**

TESTIMONIALS

IBC enables me to access the source of my life. This feeling of being home, being complete, belonging and deeply connected to the world and myself has never left me since then. It is always present and alive. From the beginning of my life, I felt that life is not complete. Life is heavy and strange. A deep "no" was ever present. I did not have a choice to this life. I felt a deep feeling of being thrown into this life just to die. Why this life? Why death? Why do I exist? Why is there so much pain here? Why shall I live in a world of pain, in a world of life and death? On a deep level in my body, I knew that this is not paradise. This part of me knew where I came from. I came from paradise. And this part will never let go of it. IBC allowed me to express all these ground-breaking realizations, feelings, discoveries. It allowed me to be held by the answers that arose. Through this process I found a way back to paradise within me. The separation ended. The separation between spirit and body collapsed into this ever present and expanding place that is impossible not to belong. It was always there. Now I can experience it and live from there any moment new, fresh and exciting. IBC is a practice to access this source daily, instantly, and effortlessly. ~ M.T.

IBC has been the hidden path that I have searched for as long as I can remember. It's so full of love, compassion, and curiosity. I can fully welcome whatever pattern, behavior, or emotional language I might be going through, and to hold it with infinite space to be explored truly, with no agenda, or specific goal. This has expanded my self-perception completely, without limits of who I am, or who I should be. The love I feel for myself has grown day by day.

Feeling free of non-judgemental thoughts and being able to explore all my beliefs in a space of love and curiosity is extraordinary. ~ A.R.

IBC has provided me with a unique experience of self-discovery and clarity in my path of personal and professional development. The technique has helped me to bring light on areas of myself that I was not paying attention to and doing so in a methodical and compassionate way. It is interesting that the IBC technique, in my experience, has no pre-established specific destination and yet asking the questions and following the process itself becomes a very powerful way upgrade "the Self" in the present moment. ~ A.S.

IBC was the beginning of my awakening towards infinite possibilities. For a long time, I was looking to learn how to free myself from my many limitations to be able to understand them, and to really be able to transcend them. IBC gave me this. IBC changed my reality. At times it was not easy, and it required going through witnessing some pain, but as I did, I found all this Zerospace already sustaining me. This space where everything is possible, where I can be myself without fear and where I accept myself as I am. IBC also taught me that depth, joy, and transformation do not end, that the path is a continuous experience of discovery. Now I live this process with the clarity of knowing that after each fall, there is more learning and I feel lighter. And of course, now my body, mind, and heart walk together. ~ P.W.

From my perspective, IBC is the most powerful methodology currently available. It is extraordinarily honest and useful, and serves to support people in finding clarity, peace, and the infinite love that already lives in each of us. In my last years using IBC, I have been able to support thousands of people to find everything they are looking for desperately outside of themselves in a deep and exciting journey, finding the most creative answers and the most powerful alignment that already lives in them. It is always available, always unlimited. Personally, when I notice confusion and stress, I just take out my phone and run the IBC App and start the journey back to Zerospace. I am deeply grateful to belong to this unique community in the world and to place this tool at the service of humanity. The world thirsts for IBC. ~ R.G.

My favorite thing about IBC is that it always knocks me for a loop. Every session. Whether I go into it looking for an answer to a quandary or simply to make myself feel better, I amazingly always end up somewhere I didn't expect. I find something I didn't know I was looking for. No one is telling me these things, rather these are realizations dragged up from the depths of me. They come from a place I don't have a name for. Short of stumbling across synchronicities or signs, this is the only process I know that gives me what I yearn for - a deep sense of ease. It has taught me that nothing needs to be difficult. ~ C.B.

It is easy, natural, for our internal conversation to go unnoticed and become background noise in our head. For years I lived that way. All these internal voices fed my daily decisions. I believe such an experience is no different from anybody else's internal dynamic. We are so invested and committed to our external world, that our voices (internal experience) are just natural noise. Some years ago I discovered the concept of IBC. What a light bulb moment. IBC shed light on my internal experience, and I became keenly aware of it. Imagine a tool you can use to question your entire internal experience to acquire a deep understanding of my own self. How do those voices drive who I become when I, for instance, believe in a certain political party? Or what kind of person am I when I prefer a particular co-worker? Why do I become strongly affected when in a discussion about a delicate subject? Questioning such things is what pointed me towards Inner-Freedom. IBC is precisely the tool that has helped me understand my internal world and the patterns that tend to be created. These patterns are usually the steppingstones I take when connecting with others; that is paramount if my desire is to build honest relationships around me. It is difficult to explain the benefits of promoting internal alignment within one-self. However, I can share, because of IBC, I have been able to, for the most part, stay true to myself. I have been able to develop compassion when connecting with others, while always honoring my boundaries. Most importantly, I live everyday with the willingness to question my internal experience once again. ~ A. J.

IBC is a powerful methodology that walks you into an inside-outside spiral that touches the depths and the vastness of our humanity, and reaches into the wisdom, light and joy of our being. IBC allows you to recognize the nature of what you are and aligns you to flow fearlessly into the world. ~ R. A.

IBC has been the way to freedom and genuine self-empowerment for me. After living my adult life mainly according to external expectations and through that creating an internal prison for myself, in IBC I found a powerful tool to listen to my heart and to all the ever so gentle voices hidden inside of me, crying to be expressed and heard. The continuous practice of IBC has been the way to a life, I truly want to live. A life of honest self-expression and authentic living deep from within in connection with much more fulfilling relationships in every aspect of my life. It helped me to overcome the internal barriers which stood in the way of my own success. ~ K. F.

IBC invites perspective and a connection to our own wisdom, leading to clarity and a way forward that honours our authentic self. It has allowed me to hold and create space for myself and for others to transform towards feeling more connected, capable and aligned. What a gift. ~ C. H.

In my experience, the IBC process offers profound opportunities for discovery and transformation. As an integrative psychotherapist, my personal IBC practice has allowed me to bring a depth and breadth to my work that was previously inaccessible. Cultivating curiosity about how the mind moves, from a place of courage and compassion has been revelatory and deeply healing. ~ C. W.

Before I knew IBC and inquiry, I was living in a small box. My life was painful and dull. I was afraid most of the time. IBC has supported me in looking behind those walls, making me realize that life is so much fun! I feel more and more connected to myself and others! It was a long process that is still going on. Having IBC in my backpack, I am safe to explore everything inside and outside. In my process, I was supported by so many fellow IBC travelers. I am very grateful and look forward to the next part of my life's journey! ~ Q. S.

IBC Is profound. With a sense of curiosity and trust in the questions, we can find answers that truly come from within. In my work as a Counsellor and in my own life, it is the one process that I return to over and over again. I know that I am never stuck with IBC and that connection to a deeper true part of myself allows for healing and freedom. ~ M. D.

I came to IBC because I was in a very challenging life situation. I hoped to get a tool with which I could solve my pain at that time. What I really experienced through IBC exceeded all my expectations: the profound experience of Zerospace! I see many spiritual teachers trying to get people to experience Zerospace, the true self. With IBC, a tool came into my life, through which I can clearly recognize my everyday thought cinema and experience the Self profoundly. A tool that enables a transformation from painful drama to deeply fulfilled self. And sometimes within a single hour! For me, IBC started a completely unexpected and incredibly intense journey. I can no longer imagine my life without it, and I am deeply grateful that I have the chance to experience it.~ M. F.

IBC has given me freedom, truth and self-confidence as a human being and coach. I've been applying this model for over six years, and I found it practical, profound, non-invasive and genuine. As an instructor, IBC has complemented my yoga and meditation practices, and I can testify to its massive impact and people's transformation on platforms such as Gympass. I've seen how C-Suite teams use IBC to experience themselves as better leaders and create assertive communication within their company. I'm proud to be part of IBC's community and excited to continue sharing the benefits of this powerful method with the world. ~ I. P.

Through IBC I realized that I had never completely arrived in my body before. The best gift of IBC for me is to have arrived, to be able to abide in myself, in my Self, to watch the world from this cozy place that is safe, and calm, and always there. Through the practice of IBC, I am able to take feelings like sadness and anger into exploration even to enjoy them – sadness becomes so cozy, anger transforms into an energy boost, joy and happiness become deep satisfaction, they fulfil me now, spread out in my body and kindle my inner light. Arriving in my body gives me stability, self-confidence and I feel anchored. My nervous system, which was ill, relaxes now. My molecules don't speed around anymore, explode wherever they want, electrify my whole body and spirit, but vibrate evenly in their specific places. There is much more peace in my life now! I am ever so grateful! ~ A. S.

IBC has been my reason to dare and feel my inner peace at the same time. The practice allowed me to avoid regrets, to be truthful to myself, to not fear my emotions but to acknowledge them, to identify what I really want in life and to step out of unpleasant situations (among many others). When I practice IBC, I feel again how the universe holds me. Every practice is a moment of understanding, of growth, of self-discovery, of a new adventure. And moreover, IBC has become part of my daily nutritionist practice with my patients. I love to be part of this community of practitioners. A true gift from and for life! ~ C. C.

The practice of IBC has had a significant impact on how I show up in the world, for myself and those around me. The core learning of this practice for me has been the practice of accessing a tool/technique/method that is in part a progressive quieting of the discoursing mind, and in part a loosening of my grip on a certain form of scepticism that overlays my mental world and my beliefs about the extent to which I am "locked into" the patterns of my thoughts. This scepticism was a barrier for me in terms of experiencing the inner state of Zerospace. Instead of trusting my innate ability to actually experience Zerospace, I engaged in a constant "future oriented" bargaining with my conviction that the same thoughts and mental discourse will simply show up again and again, tomorrow and the next day. It was not until I could let go of this and allow myself the privilege to actually experience a state of "nothing left" in the mental chatter, that I was able to experience the alignment of my nervous system and mental state. In so doing, I learned to trust in the experience and the fact that Zerospace seems to transform me and that this has lasting impact in my mental, emotional, and "bodily" world. ~ M. M.

ORGANIZATIONAL RESULTS WITH IBC

When looking into organizational/business results using IBC, overall improvements in leadership traits were considerable in all categories that we have formally assessed. The most improved leadership trait was the quality of **Presence** (being fully available to meet the needs of arising situations), where an average **136%** improvement was reported. The quality of **Openness** (accepting and owning personal areas of growth and opportunity) came in at **114%**. *Enthusiasm* (looking for opportunity in difficult situations) came in at **87%**. *Courageousness* (trusting yourself and team without giving into fear) came in at **84%**. *Receptiveness*, (listening to others before making decisions) came in at **83%**.

To learn more about our results and our evaluation methodologies feel free to visit **innerland.com**

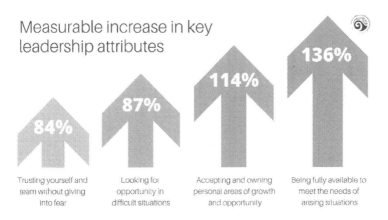

Figure 1: Measurable increase in key leadership attributes

Figure 2: Individual markers after one year of practice

Leadership Trait	Groups 1 & 2:	Category
Enthusiast	87.01	
Clear	55.45	**Engagement**
Committed	30.21	**57.55%**
Flexible	82.12	
Courageous	83.85	**Adaptability**
Open	113.75	**93.24%**
Appreciative	61.95	
Receptive	82.88	
Patient	63.41	
Respectful	74.30	**Collegiality**
Trusting	56.39	**67.79%**
Present	136.18	
Responsible	66.02	**Integrity**
Equitable	82.05	**94.75%**
Overall Improvement	**76.83%**	

Figure 3: Overall improvement in one year of practice.

Innerland Institute

Currently, at the Innerland Institute we offer IBC Certification programs for coaches and therapists as well as leadership development programs for organizations. We also offer short introduction courses as well long-term immersion programs for the general public including life-changing retreats in incredible locations. We also offer our two-year Innerland Institute Coaching certification program as well as one-on-one coaching for individuals.

IBC TRAINING AND CERTIFICATION

We offer training and certification in IBC for coaches, counsellors, social workers, therapists, consultants, or other professionals in similar fields that already have experience holding space for clients supporting them towards their goals.

The full IBC Certification process consists of four sets of two-day workshops that are offered fully online. These two-day workshops need to be taken in sequence and within two years, nevertheless these courses can also be taken in isolation for personal learning purposes only.

After completing the first two-day program participants can call themselves "IBC informed". Full certification will be awarded after the completion of the four training courses. For availability and dates please visit **innerland.com**

The 4 IBC Certification courses are:

I: IBC & Zerospace (2 days)
II: IBC & Relationships (2 days)
III: IBC & Purpose (2 days)
IV: IBC & Parts (2 days)

BECOMING AN INNERLAND COACH™

If you have no previous training in supporting others, you can become an **Innerland Coach™** by completing two years of training at the Innerland Institute **(innerland.com)**. This program consists of 400 hours of training and practice that will give you the confidence to be able to support and facilitate others in their process of transformation and alignment. This program offers full training and certification on IBC as well. This program is available to all individuals regardless of professional background or previous training.

IBC FOR PERSONAL PRACTICE

We offer several programs for individuals that want to learn, experience and practice IBC for their own personal benefit and transformation through the **Innerland Institute (innerland.com).** These programs are offered to the general public without any expectation of previous training or experience. Some of these programs include:

Innerland Immersion: This is a yearly program that gives participants the opportunity to immerse and practice access, sustainment, and expansion to Zerospace in community with others for the purposes of their own healing and self-transformation. Some immersions can be taken fully online, and some may include face to face retreats.

Innerland Workshops and Retreats: Additionally, we offer several programs and retreats, ranging from two days to two weeks. These programs are also designed to offer the direct experience of accessing, relaxing into and expanding Zerospace so that you can learn the models and start moving towards your full embodiment of Zerospace.

One-On-One Coaching and Support: The Innerland Institute additionally offers services for individuals that would like personalized support through personalized coaching on how to identify, relax into, and live from Zerospace.

IBC App: We additionally have the IBC App available in both IOS and Android. Search for "Innerland" or "ibc" on your app store.

LEADERSHIP DEVELOPMENT PROGRAMS FOR ORGANIZATIONS

Our corporate programs are individually tailored to the needs of each organization. We have already presented the results of these programs in the previous section showing the amazing results we've had. For further information about our leadership development programs for organizations please visit **innerland.com** we will be happy to set up a time to explore your needs.

The Innerland Institute was co-founded in 2003 by Tania Fierro and Pedro Cortina and has served thousands of individuals to date. For the last several years at the Innerland Institute, we have been offering one-on-one life and executive coaching, workshops, retreats, and immersion programs specializing in Inquiry-Based methodologies.

As of today, we are truly impressed with the extraordinary results we are seeing at a personal and organizational level arising from the implementation of IBC. As of this date, we have been able to bring IBC into the lives of countless individuals as well as into the meeting rooms and board rooms of several important organizations. We have also offered programs all around the world in cities such as Toronto, Calgary, Vancouver, New York, Los Angeles, Philadelphia, Mexico City, Zurich, Dublin, Cadiz, Indianapolis, St Louis, Los Cabos, San Miguel Allende, Merida, Tulum, and Playa del Carmen amongst others.

About the Authors

ABOUT TANIA

Tania Fierro, MA is a speaker, author, philosophical counselor, coach, facilitator, management consultant, Olympic athlete and transformation specialist with more than 20 years of experience in the field of inquiry-based transformation. Since co-founding the Innerland Institute in 2003, she has been offering clients a deeply compassionate, razor-sharp awareness that gets to the crux of any situation. She is also co-developer of the IBC process. There is no issue that Inquiry cannot hold, and she invites us not to believe her and to try it for ourselves. Tania describes herself as a philosopher in the most literal sense of being "a lover of wisdom", in this case, supporting inner wisdom. She is also a Certified Counselor by the American Philosophical Practitioners Association in New York and undertook training on Foundations of IFS at the Adler Graduate Professional School in Toronto. She is also the former director for the Institute of The Work.

She holds bachelor's and master's degrees in philosophy and ethics. She was a participant in the 1988 Seoul Olympics and served as the Human Rights Director at Tibet House Mexico. Tania has 20 years of experience supporting individuals and organizations in questioning and undoing the repetitive, stressful patterns that cause suffering and blocks in our lives. Throughout her life, she has been fully immersed in several eastern transformational traditions such as Mahamudra, Dzogchen, and Advaita. Tania has a very successful coaching and counselling practice and travels the world offering training and workshops in IBC.

ABOUT PEDRO

Dr. Pedro Cortina is an author, master coach, speaker, counselor, facilitator, philosopher, trainer, transformation specialist as well as an entrepreneurship and leadership expert with more than 20 years of experience. He offers a profound space of exploration and grounding to identify and transform what is getting in the way of our passion, purpose and success. He is the co-founder of the Innerland Institute as well as co-developer of the IBC™ model. He is also the author of the book *Curflexion*, a guide for moving away from our underlying human experience of separation and unfulfillment.

He holds a bachelor's degree in philosophy and economics as well as masters and doctoral degrees specializing in leadership and entrepreneurship from the University of British Columbia and the University of Calgary. He is also a certified counselor by the American Philosophical Practitioners Association in New York, a graduate of the Certificate in Applied IFS Therapy and Broader Clinical Applications at the Adler Graduate Professional School in Toronto and a graduate of the Finance Program for Senior

Executives at the University of Oxford. Additionally, throughout his life, he has been fully immersed in several eastern transformational traditions such as Mahamudra, Dzogchen, and Advaita.

innerland.com

THE IBC APP IS AVAILABLE FOR IOS/ANDROID

Manufactured by Amazon.ca
Bolton, ON